Author Richard Green has nearly 40 years in the cheese trade, mainly as a cheese grader and also a judge at many local, national and international cheese shows.

Starting out with what was Europe's largest farmhouse cheddar cheese store in Wells, he gained his experience at grading and selecting cheese, while over the years also experienced all aspects from actually making the cheese to working in the pre-packing rooms.

Working for one of the well known traditional farmhouse cheddar cheese makers, seeing how regulations and to a degree politics had an effect on this and many other family businesses, not to mention the might of the massive national and international cheese companies, is told in this book, and often, not always for the best to the family concerns.

While this book not only gives a history of cheddar cheese making in the West Country, with its origins based around England's smallest city of Wells in Somerset, it also deals with the highs and lows of a product which is now made and available throughout the world.

Due to many factors, which this book will highlight, from a total of around 1,000 cheese makers there are only around 10 farmhouse cheddar cheese makers left in the West Country.

Against a background of turmoil and change, glimmers of hope are given by those who are left, who continue to diversify in the industry, along with a new era of artisan cheese makers, whom the author has got to know over the years, and in turn is seeing history start to repeat itself.

The LAST West Country Cheddar Cheese Makers

Richard Green

First Edition: The LAST West Country Cheddar Cheese Makers

First published in Great Britain in 2015 by:
Tamar Books
24 Forest Houses
Halwill
Beaworthy
EX21 5UU
www.indigodreams.co.uk

ISBN 978-0-9574742-2-2
Tamar Books is an imprint of Indigo Dreams Publishing Ltd

Designed and typeset in Times New Roman by Indigo Dreams.

Cover photograph James Keen ©the Keen family.

Printed and bound in Great Britain by 4edge Ltd
www.4edge.co.uk

Papers used by Indigo Dreams are recyclable products made from wood grown in sustainable forests following the guidance of the Forest Stewardship Council.

CONTENTS

FOREWORD

I remember as a child the importance of the cheese grader's monthly visit to the farm. At stake was Father's income, the cheese maker's pride and the happiness of the whole farming household. The cheese had to be judged the finest quality Farmhouse Cheddar to receive the magenta oval stamp or its sale would be unprofitable and the farm's reputation diminished. Richard Green followed in the line of such Cheese Graders as Messrs Dicker, Howe, and Plenty separating the very best and the good from the mediocre.

In this history Richard brings to life the characters who made Cheddar the world's favourite cheese. The production of Cheddar has been so successful that it is now concentrated in a few dairies. Richard relates how this has happened. He retells the stories that he has collected and researched and those from his own experience working in the Farmhouse Cheddar industry.

The beginning of this story is Milk, an elixir for good life from suckling to old age. The traditional cheese makers drew on their experience, their own alchemy, to produce cheese with flavours and textures that remain in the memory. Richard continues his story introducing the new generation of Artisan cheese makers who are relearning the craft of preserving the glories of raw milk in cheese.

As with bread, beer and cured meat there is now a great variety of interesting cheeses, so many that you can taste a different British cheese every day of the year if you have the enthusiasm to search them out. So settle down with a piece of raw milk Cheddar, an apple and a glass of Somerset cider and read this intriguing and continuing story of Somerset Cheddar cheese makers!

George Keen

INTRODUCTION

The times I have been asked over the years to write a book about cheddar cheese and the cheese makers of Somerset has finally come, and with the numbers of family businesses ever decreasing, now is the moment.

Having been in the business covering all aspects from cheese making to cheese grading and judging, to the mundane officialdom of audits, there is a story to be told.

Over the years, too much trivial and false portrayals have not helped the real world of cheese making, and while 'cheese' and 'cider' have helped to market the image of Somerset, this in turn has been a missed marketing opportunity that has not been fully realised to its full potential.

Even, in England's smallest city of Wells, in the heart of the rural county, not only did it have its own cheese making dairy but also the largest 'traditional' cheese store in Europe, while the former is still part of Palace Farm, but used for other farm purposes, the latter succumbed to housing, while just across the road, another dairy related plant of Cow and Gate, later known as Nutricia was totally modernised; yet within a short space of time, this was also demolished and to be replaced by more housing!

After the Second World War, there were over 1,000 small farmhouse cheese makers, and when I joined the Milk Marketing Board, at their delightful sounding cheese factors of Crump, Way Ltd, there were around 30 left, and these small band of artisans were to continue shrinking in size, to today when there are only 10 left.

It is not all doom and gloom, as I have been lucky to be part of the Specialist Cheese makers Association since its inception to have seen the rise of the much smaller new era of artisan cheese makers, not just making a whole range of cheeses, but made from various milks, such as buffalo, ewes and goats.

As part of the Specialist Cheese makers Association, I have also been part of a new age of Cheese Show, with our first outing at Butler's

Wharf, Tower Bridge in London, with this event developing into the start of the British Cheese Awards, which I have had the privilege to judge at many times.

There have been many highs and lows over the years, which will become apparent in the ensuing pages, having met many carnival princesses, royal princesses, though the highlight for myself was being asked to do a judging demonstration for her Majesty the Queen, at the Centenary event of the Devon County Show.

Along the way, I have the pleasure to work alongside some of the doyens of the cheese world, most notably Miss K. D. Maddever whom I enjoyed taking around some of the farms, to "see her boys!"

As most large conglomerate businesses have adapted to the world stage, some of the county's larger cheese makers have become more market orientated, while some have been swallowed up by other multi-national companies and it is brands like 'Cathedral City' that still have a link to the county's small city, by way of their logo depicting the west front of Wells Cathedral.

While there are only a few original farmhouse cheddar cheese makers now surviving, there is still a future, and while it may be more in keeping with our technological computerised age, often exasperated by the fickle world of politics, some makers such as the Keen's of Wincanton and Montgomery's of North Cadbury are to be praised for keeping to their unpasteurised roots, while equally Ashley Chase down in Dorset, are to be noted for their caved aged cheddar, thanks in part to the shared marketing of entrepreneurial Showman Gerry Cottle and his visitor attraction, Wookey Hole caves near Wells and the marketing prowess of Mike Pullin, a Director for Barbers of Ditcheat.

Yes, I admit it, I am a staunch traditionalist, though I gather many people, already knew that, and I know how preservationists such as late Fred Dibnah and late Michael Oliver feel over such strong Victorian values, which are certainly much better than the disposable attitudes and values of today's modern era.

So much of what put the 'Great' into 'Britain', has passed away into the pages of our history books, or are to be found in exhibits of their era in static museums.

We have seen our coal mining, car making, fishing, steel industry, ship building and many other aspects decline over the years, and now our farmhouse cheddar cheese makers down to such small levels; hence another reason for putting this book together, couple with the fact that being born in Wells, cheese has had large impact on my life, and as you are becoming aware, England's smallest city, was for a long time an integral part of the heritage and history of West Country Farmhouse Cheddar cheese.

"The true home town of cheddar is Wells", is quoted by T.A.Layton in his cheese handbook of 1957, and unlike so many so called articles written on cheese, by a myriad of food writers over the years, this book is purely based on known facts about the heritage of West Country Farmhouse cheddar.

A good West Country Farmhouse Cheddar, should be ripened for between 9 and 12 months of age and have keeping qualities, to be deemed as mature.

Connoisseurs who prefer something stronger, can look out for terms such as 'extra mature' and 'vintage' being that the cheese is kept upwards to 18 months or more.

Local variations in milk, produced by a combination of local soil, grass and different breeds of cattle, add up to the individual characteristics of West Country Farmhouse Cheddar.

Flavours which are acidic or sharper are not genuine mature flavours, likewise tangy or twangy flavours are again not authentic, but are simply myths.

While such modern ambiguities stating mature can be mellow and mild with a mature flavour are inaccurate and detrimental.

Mature is mature, there is no substitute.

Unfortunately and unrealistically, there are still some individuals who have scant regard for the true characteristics of West Country Farmhouse Cheddar, and look for fictitious and demeaning flavours such as 'farmyard flavour' or 'the cows tail'.

These misconceptions are not only extremely offensive, they are seriously dangerous in our health conscious age.

On the most positive side, in securing a future for the farmhouse cheese makers that are left, is that West Country Farmhouse Cheddar is now protected by the P.D.O., being the Protected Designation of Origin, safeguarding it has a part of our English heritage.

To conclude this introduction, it is fitting to leave with a statement over the P.D.O., and for all those who have contributed in one form or another to this publication, a full list will be found in the acknowledgements at the end of the book.

Philip Crawford, former Chairman, of the West Country Farmhouse Cheese makers, stated, "The logo, which will be recognised throughout Europe as a symbol of quality, has been welcomed by all those who have suffered from the exploitative practices of copy-cat companies. Protecting the tradition of cheddar making in the West Country is very important. There are too many farmhouse imitation brands of cheddar coming out of creameries which threaten to dilute the quality of real farmhouse cheddar."

Richard Green

The LAST West Country Cheddar Cheese Makers

CHEESE TO MARKET

"Cheese making is one of the very oldest crafts indeed, 'cheese of kind' , is mentioned in the Bible, and there is evidence that cheese was made in this country at the time of the Roman occupation", quotes the formidable and most respected doyen of the last century of cheese making, the late, Miss K.D.Maddever.

This book relates largely to the county of Somerset, while occasional trips over the borders to Devon to the Quicke family near Exeter and the Willes family near Bideford and into Dorset to the Streatfeild Hood family near Bridport will be accounted from time to time.

The county of Somerset, has a long history, and has become world renown for both its cheese and cider making, and this book is an attempt to differentiate the realities from the myths of the folklore associated with the history of farmhouse cheddar.

Looking back over the years, the first recorded evidence of farm made cheese being made, was to be found in the far south east of the county, at the hamlet of Charlton Horethorne, which in turn is situated on the edge of the Blackmore Vale.

It was here in 1086, that 100 such farm made cheeses were each sold for 3 shillings and 6d, and to put this into some form of perspective, when inflation has made price comparisons virtually meaningless, a farm labourer of that period of time, would barely earn a penny a day!

Interestingly, the 100 cheese returned £17 and 10 shillings at 1086 prices, while over a 100 years later prices for cheddar would increase at markets with £11 being paid for 40 cheddars, while in 1184, one of King John's sons paid £10 for 40 cheddars!

Also at this time, other basic foodstuffs such as eggs were a penny a dozen and local made ale was a penny a gallon!

From the famous village, nestling under the Mendip Hills, with its unique Gorge, the Cheddar Parish Records dealing with issues related to cheese, and its first known evidence calling the product, cheddar cheese, it was in 1170, when King Henry the Second, bought 80 hundredweights for £11!

Later, records of Caerphilly and Cheddar cheeses, made by the farmers of the county's villages and towns in the 1200's, were mainly sold at the Highbridge and Wells markets and fairs, while in Dorset, Beaminster and Woodbury Hill were the principal venues.

The people looking after the transportation and distribution of the cheeses, were known as 'Cheese Jobbers', who in turn sold the parcels of cheese on, at other notable fairs, such as Reading in Berkshire and Winchester St. Giles Fair in Hampshire, for their final marketing on the principal trade routes into London.

How much actual tonnage of cheese was distributed in those long off days can only be assumed? But bearing in mind at this point of time, Cheshire cheese which was mainly made in the county of the same name, along with being produced in Lancashire, Shropshire and Staffordshire; have recorded evidence of 14,000 tons of Cheshire cheese alone, being transported by the 'Cheese Jobbers' on route to London, with the majority going by river cargo along the rivers Severn and Trent for most of the journey.

After the ravages of the 'Black Death', and the start of the One Hundred Years War with France, it was needless to say, agriculture and other labourers were very thin on the ground, and it was no wonder there was to be a 'Peasants Revolt'.

Toll charges for fairs and markets, were also expensive during this period, such as a horse and cart load of produce would cost a penny and just a horse load of goods at half a penny, while for a man carrying all he could, the charge would be, one farthing.

Livestock prices were also at a high of an average 12 shillings and 6d per cow, 3 shillings and 6d a pig and for a horse the price was around 13 shillings and 6d, set against a background labourers pay being a 1d a day, which would rise up to 2d a day at harvest time.

By the 1400's, Glastonbury farmers are recorded to be getting 5 shillings and 6d for farm made cheese at the local markets, and while it commanded a high price, mainly for the 'cheddar' types of cheese; for a quick turnaround in cash flow, Caerphilly and Cheshire cheeses, were still the predominate made.

In 1557, the famous agricultural journalist, known as Tusser, wrote a rhyme for the benefit of a warning to one of his dairymaids, called Cisley

'Gassy cheese full of eyes'

'If cheese in dairy have Argus his eyes,
Tell Cisley, the fault in her housewifery lies'

'Cheese too salt'

'Leave Lot with his pillar, good Cisley alone,
Much saltiness in whitemeat is ill for the stone'

Cheese Doyens: Marc Adams on the left with Arthur Hamilton on the right with the author in the centre at the Royal Bath and West Show.

If some cheddar cheeses were having faults with openness and too much salting, another fault of dryness was being stated by William Camden, the English antiquarian, in his book 'Brittania', quoting the cheddar tasted "like parmesan in flavour", and being in weight, "so heavy, it took two men to lift them."

Another writer of the time, called Fuller, cites of the cheddar being "so expensive, it could only be found on the tables of the rich."

The more known writer, Samuel Pepys, also added his thoughts on the cheddar, by balancing out the criticisms, that despite the costs and weights, "cheddar was still very popular."

In the Market Place of Wells in the 1600's, records are available that show over 100 tons of farm made cheddar were sold on a yearly basis, with the space in the inverted L shape market area, soon to be known as the 'Open Cheese Market', and proving so economical this was to carry on well into the 1800's.

Prices around this period of time were documented as 75 shillings per hundredweight, while for the smaller 'truckles of cheddar', were to fetch about 5 shillings per hundredweight.

Around this period of time, there were early forms of consumer protection, which were a lot more, stricter, and severe, with bakers who sold substandard products being flogged in the streets, while fishmongers and butchers were put into nearby stocks, and had their condemned produce, burned beneath their noses!

Somerset, by now in the 1600's was proving itself as the county for the farm made cheddars of distinction, proven by the visit of King Charles the First, secretary Viscount Conway, who ordered two cheddars to be sent to the king.

Due to a misunderstanding, only one such farm made cheddar was sent, and in the Kings angry response, Viscount Conway was sent back to Somerset, to "rake up all the cheeses at Cheddar for himself."

In 1635, Lord Poulett apologised to the Kings secretary, making what could be an excuse stating, "this is all that can be gotten of last summer's making," going on to add, "I will take care to victual him (*King Charles*) better against another winter."

Probably, as a safeguard for such an embarrassment repeating itself, the local farmers of Cheddar, were to create what could be deemed as the very first 'co-operative' in 1666, though it was more probably a communal group, and was known as the 'Cheddar Club'.

Later during 1724, the village of Cheddar, was to be given another small piece of its importance to the origins of the cheese's history, by way of the visit of Daniel Defoe, forming part of his trilogy of books entitled, 'A Tour Through The Whole Island Of Great Britain', whereupon he was to say of the increasingly popular dairy product. "It is in my opinion, the best cheese that England affords, if not the whole world affords."

Daniel Defoe, also quotes that prices being paid for Cheddar, were '6d to 8d a pound' while for Cheshire, it was '2d a pound'.

According to the Cheddar Parish Records, 'the cheese was without doubt taken from the village of Cheddar, which through its cliffs and caves was the most famous of all Somerset landmarks from earliest times."

The term 'taken' is open to question for defining, but the Parish Records go on to add, 'It is certain that the mode of making this cheese; cheddar cheese, was not to be confined to the village boundaries, but to all the villages nestling under the base of the Mendip Hills'.

Adding credence to these facts, the cheddar cheese made at Bridgwater was to be called either Bridgwater Cheddar or Bridgwater Double Gloucester, for little attention was paid or adhered to trade description in these times, and equally weights and measures were unheard of, for the weight of the cheddars ranged from 100 pounds (50 kilos) to 150 pounds (75 kilos) per cheese, making the task of the 'Cheese Jobbers' even more arduous, as noted in 1772.

Such disregard for the authorities, was to be stated in a report for 1794, by the then version of a department for agriculture, quoting 'little attention was paid to cheese and butter', though the report does confirm that the 'cheddar making area, was centered around Axbridge, Cheddar, Glastonbury, Shepton Mallet, Wells and the Mendip Hills'.

Against this background, the two consecutive years of 1777 and 1778, were to be well documented in the cheddar cheese world, for in 1777, Edmund Rack formed what is today's Royal Bath and West Show Society, while in 1778, Joseph Harding was born, whom as these pages will later inform, was to have a major impact on the actual cheddar cheese making procedures.

Before both individuals were to make their longer lasting impressions, the cheddar cheese prices which had remained at high levels since the early 1700's, were to take a major tumble in 1826, dropping by as much as 20% to 50%, despite the fact, only two thirds of the previous 1825 production had been made.

By the mid 1850's, the prices recovered and vastly improved, rising from 66 shillings per hundredweight in 1850, up to 70 shillings per hundredweight in 1852, and up once more in 1853 to 75 shillings per hundredweight.

With cheese prices continuing an overall rise, a new form of business was slowly being introduced by way of private auction taking over from public bartering, and as such, this aspect of commodities, began to fade away from the cheese fairs and markets around Britain.

In contrast to this change of format, the Royal Bath and West Show Society, was formed by Edmund Rack, which saw the rise in a new form of a yearly agriculture event, and others in the Somerset area, soon followed, such as the Mid Somerset Show at Shepton Mallet commencing in 1832, the North Somerset Show beginning in 1856, and the aptly named Frome Cheese Show originating in 1877.

It is from the Bath and West Journal of 1857, that the very first accurate description of 'cheddar' is mentioned, when the Ayrshire Agriculture Association came to Somerset to see methods of cheddar cheese making.

Joseph Harding, who gave his name to the process of 'cheddaring' the curds from the whey in its manufacture, came from the village of Compton Dando, just to the south of Bath, described the 'new' process to the gathered delegation, along with his other ideas based on the unique recipe.

Miss K.D.Maddever, sums up this period of time, "Joseph Harding of Compton Dando in Somerset did much original work to 'improve' cheddar cheese", going on to add in one of her letters, "His sons travelled the world teaching cheese making and one settled in Australia. What a pity we didn't 'trademark' the name 'cheddar' cheese only; cheddar cheese is now made throughout the world."

How so many of us echo her statements, when even today there is often so much cheap inferior so called cheddar to be had, often imported into this country.

Also casting a shadow over cheese making in the 1850's, was the transportation of liquid milk by the up and coming railway network, making the seven day labour of cheese making expensive, for the liquid market for milk was being more profitable in comparison.

To start counteracting these changing market conditions, it was around this period of time, that along with the larger size cheddar cheeses, which were still weighing in at around 70 to 120 pound; due to the historical fact that the process was to make all of each days milk per farm of around 30 to 40 cows into one single cheese.

Cheesemaking course at Reaseheath College, Nantwich, Cheshire in 1999, with the remarkable Val Bines

It is in this point of time, that the first stated 'truckles' of cheddar cheese became to be known, with them weighing in at around 10 to 15 pound (5 kilos), and consequently demand for them quickly grew, being sold to a wider range of families for their convenience of size, and were to be very popular being sold at Chippenham (Wiltshire) and at Highbridge markets.

From the 1850's up to the 1890's, the average price for this new shape and weight of cheddar, was around 5 shillings per hundredweight.

As the 1800's were coming to a close; dramatic changes were happening at the height of the Victorian era, for the 'Industrial Revolution' brought with it, the power of 'steam', and as said, helped to speed up the distribution of the liquid milk market, while in 1870, England's very first cheese factory opened up for production at Longford in Derbyshire, and within five more years, 10 more cheese factories were to be in manufacture throughout all of England.

With such an abundance of cheese being made, it was not surprising to see a collapse of the cheese market, particularly for Cheddar and Cheshire types of cheeses, with quotes of 72 shillings per hundredweight in 1885; which with shipping also now a global means of transportation; American imports were bringing prices down, and while Canadian cheese was somewhat scarce, there was also a good supply of New Zealand cheese, while closer to English shores, Dutch Gouda cheese was also in short supply, culminating in 1899 that English cheese prices had spiralled down to 44 shillings per hundredweight.

With a growing background of quantity than quality in cheese making, the loyal Somerset farmhouse cheese makers struggled on with their time honoured traditional ways of manufacture, and it was during the price collapse era, in 1890, that the Bath and West Show Society sponsored the very first Cheese School, though such notable families as the Candy and Cannons were at first, very reluctant to give any trade secrets of their recipes away, of their cheese making procedures.

The very first Cheddar cheese school, was set up on May 1st 1890, at the Palace Farm in Wells, under the shadow of the famous landmarks the Cathedral and the Bishop's Palace, being sanctioned by the Ecclesiastical Commissioners, with the then tenant of the farm being Mr E.C.Wickham, with the cheese making supervised by Henry Cannon, whom himself originated from Milton Clevedon, near Evercreech, just a few miles away to the east of England's smallest city.

Fees for the students at this time, which included board and lodging, were £3 and three shillings, with most of the students coming from a farming background.

Cheese production at the school began on May 6th and continued on up to October 31st, with the fruits of their labour being purchased later by Hill Brothers of Evercreech, with prices fetching 63 shillings per hundredweight; which worked at around 6d a pound in weight! While, overall considering the general market conditions, this was not a bad achievement.

In total, 174 hundredweight of cheddar cheese was made by the first intake of students!

After the opening of the first cheese school in the county at Wells, others were soon to follow, such as at Vallis Farm near Frome in 1891, and Compton House Farm at Axbridge in 1892.

Such was the good quality of the cheese, that at the local Evercreech and Frome Shows, in the dairy sections, the students had a most encouraging start, by winning many prize cards for all their hard work.

More local cheese schools, were soon to follow, such as in 1906, at Glendale Farm in Wedmore, owned by the then Porter family, and in 1907, at Dudwell Farm in Chewton Mendip, when owned by the Dewdney family.

Cheese Record books, were meticulously looked after; such as by one student named Florence Hooper, who originated from Stowell Farm at Sherborne in Dorset.

Everything was precisely recorded, right from the number of cows milked (then 60 in total), temperatures of the weather conditions, all aspects of the cheese manufacturing procedures, carrying on through to the amounts made and storage conditions; making not only fascinating reading in its own right, but this was to be the forerunner of today's 'due diligence' and 'transparent traceability' regimes.

As the 1900's progressed, uniformity of size, shape and weight of the cheddar cheeses were still major problems of manufacture, ranging from the 'truckles', weighing in at around 15 to 20 pound (5 to 10 kilos), while the larger cheeses ranged from between 70 to 100 pound (35 to 50 kilos), and some even at a mighty one and a half hundredweight (over 70 kilos!).

One particular cheddar cheese, known locally in Somerset, as the 'Great Pennard Cheese' of 1839, weighed a massive half a ton, and will be told at length in the next chapter, while its 1989 counterpart, the 'Second Great Pennard Cheese', made by the Green family of West Pennard, near Glastonbury, will also be given some coverage.

During the First World War of 1914 to 1918, farmhouse cheese making was to be very uneconomical, with the larger retail dairies, reducing prices at very notices and often returned the unsold milk! In all, during the hostilities, farmhouse cheese including that of cheddar, virtually ceased production, apart from own local sales at the farm gate or the nearest market.

It was during these bleak times, that one farming family, the Greens of West Pennard, against the odds, started their cheese making business in 1916, though on a very small scale.

John Green, recalls these times by stating, "Cheddar cheese at this time, was made by farmers wives and local girls, with the season starting in April and ending in September, with the cheese produced from the cheap summer grass", going on to add, "The girls were known as dairymaids, and were trained over two seasons, with the first year, they paid to undertake the work! While in the second year they were known as 'improvers' and earned £16 at the end of September!"

Without doubt these were very hard times, with John Green also recalling that "Not only did the dairymaids make the cheese, they also helped to milk the cows and did household chores-seven days a week!" As for the marketing of the local cheddar cheese, John Green remembers, "When the cheddar season finished, Caerphilly cheese was sometimes made, which was taken by my father to the weekly Highbridge market, where it was sold to dealers, with the cheese then being railed to South Wales where it was very popular with the coal miners, being a good digestible food."

Against a background of these hard troubled times, and trying to get some form of unity and conformity into the farmhouse cheese making world; it was finally in 1927, that the first organised attempts of 'cheese grading' were introduced, with the formation of the Cheshire Cheese Federation and the English Cheddar Cheese Federation, along with collectively marketing the cheeses.

To help the farmhouse cheese makers in the Somerset area, Archdeacon Denison from East Brent, near Highbridge; whom himself, had also helped originate Somerset's unique 'Harvest Home' festivities, also stood up to fight the cause, by pledging his full support for the farmhouse cheddar industry, stating, "I am glad to fight for dear old cheddar cheese."

It was finally in 1933, that the Milk Marketing Board was formed, to help restore security for the English and Welsh farmers, including the remaining 1,500 farmhouse cheese makers who were now in serious difficulties.

Also in 1933, the introduction of the 'National Mark' scheme, was incorporating the Cheshire and English Cheddar cheese schemes, particularly over quality assurance, while shortly afterwards in 1937, other English farm made cheeses and factory creamery types of cheese were also incorporated into the 'National Mark' scheme.

During this period of time, under the Milk Marketing Board, the 1,500 farmhouse cheese makers were producing overall in total, only a quarter of the cheese sold that was actually made in Britain, with 514 farmhouse makers producing Cheddar and Caerphilly in the counties of Devon, Dorset, Somerset and Wiltshire, while 405 farmhouse makers manufactured Cheshire in Cheshire and Lancashire, while the remaining 581 farmhouse cheese makers were spread throughout the remaining counties of England and Wales, making other regional types of what are known as 'territorial cheeses', such as Caerphilly ,Derby, Double Gloucester, Lancashire, Red Leicester, Stilton and Wensleydale.

This seemingly appropriate get together of farmhouse cheese makers came just before the Second World War of 1939 to 1945, which was to cause even more devastation to an already beleaguered farming community of Britain.

John Green, in one of his papers sums up these trouble times " While there was 'certainty' of milk being sold to the Milk Marketing Board, and the growing number of factories centralizing cheese making, many farmers gave up cheese making, which led to further contraction of farmhouse manufacture."

Royal Visit To Devon County's Centenary Show 1995 with the author meeting H.R.H. The Queen

In 1940, the then government, set up the 'Ministry of Food', which became the sole purchaser of cheese under a compulsory scheme; the organisation being created to help the nations diet, and for farmhouse cheese making, this was to be yet another major setback, for all milk had to go to the country's factories, being better known as 'creameries' which turned the milk into hard pressed cheeses.

The two World Wars, also hit the farming community workforce, with the period of time now seeing the farmers wives and other women becoming the linchpins to uphold the craft of farmhouse cheese making, and due to the such uneconomical conditions, what farm made cheeses there were, these were only sold locally; for the collection and delivery of such wartime restrictions on fuel, were also another serious consequence on their demise due to such distribution problems.

Even at the local markets, the shortages of cheese, made the venues desolate places, with only the quick ripening cheeses being the main products for sale; such as at Highbridge, under the gavel of auctioneers W.H.Palmer and Son, receiving each Tuesday, between 50 and 100 tons of Caerphilly cheese between the two world war conflicts; but during the Second World War itself, none if any Caerphilly was made on a significant scale, and the market had no option other than to close.

In 1948, three years after the war had ended, it is recorded that only 44 of the 405 Cheshire cheese makers remained in operation, while only 61 of the 514 Cheddar and Caerphilly farmhouse cheese makers were still in production, the majority now in Devon, Dorset and Somerset.

Though the Ministry of Agriculture and the Milk Marketing Board began to slowly revive the ailing farmhouse cheese making industry, post wartime rationing and price restrictions were still to be major obstacles, though the factory creameries did manage to produce some unpasteurised cheeses.

In 1955, saw the formation of the National Association of Creamery Proprietors and Wholesale Dairymen, created to grade creamery made cheese, while in the same year, the Milk Marketing Board, formed the Farmhouse Cheese maker's scheme, to grade farm made cheeses, along with agents being appointed to market the cheeses.

Quite why T.A.Layton quoted, "The true home town of cheddar is Wells" in his 1957 publication. 'The Cheese Handbook' is open for interpretation? Had such a remark been made in 1964, then it would have, without question not be debated, for in the period up to this time, the Milk Marketing Board had carried out a major review of its structure of the business, and created what was to be a then for its age, a state of the art, central temperature controlled store, situated on the southern edge of the cathedral city, being fully operational in 1964, and was regarded as the then 'largest traditional cheese cold store in Europe', about the size of two football pitches.

Based at Keward Farm, the premises were under the auspices of Crump Way and Company, who up to this point of time, had used a wide variety of contrasting storage premises, many in old antiquated buildings, around the city at Market Street and Southover.

In its early years, row upon row, with many as 10 shelves high with 8 farm made round cheddars per shelve, would be matured by the farmhouse cheese makers agents, with the store split into 3 main sections, with the 'traditional' area consisting of 4 stores with each holding around 20,000 farm cloth bound made cheddars, making around 80,000 such cheeses.

The second area, again, of 4 stores, were now of the creamery influence of packaging the farmhouse cheddars, being in block form as opposed to round shape, making them easier for cutting and packing for the growing rise of the supermarkets. As opposed to 20,000 per round cheese store, there were now 40,000 block style cheddars per store, making a total of 160,000 block made farmhouse cheddars; making a joint total over 240,000 cheeses.

While the block cheddars were averaging 40 pound (20 kilos) in weight, the round cheddars were still variable being between 50 to 60 pound (25 to 30 kilos), along with a few still being made in the 100 pound (50 kilos) size range!

Being such hard work and labour intensive and more for the male workforce, in the large cold store, staff were to be hard to get hold of, and there were many times when local 'out patients' from the city's Mendip Hospital, and even 'prisoners' from nearby Shepton Mallet were brought in to help clean and turn the seemingly endless numbers of cheeses.

The third area of the building was for a packing room section, for not only did the cheese go out whole to the distributors , wholesalers and other packers, Crump Way also had its own packing lines for two brands that were born in the city, being 'Bishops Reserve' and the fast growing popularity of 'Cathedral City'. The workforce here were mainly female, with a few men cutting the whole cheese down into more manageable sizes for pre packing.

By the mid 1970's, with market conditions constantly changing, largely due to the spread of supermarkets across Britain, only 22 of the 44 Cheshire farmhouse cheese makers remained in business, while mainly in

Somerset, only 33 of the 61 farmhouse Cheddar makers were in manufacture.

It was at this point of time, when the author joined Crump Way, and was to embark on a journey into the world of farmhouse cheddar cheese making, and to be fortunate to cover all aspects of the business.

While the farmhouse cheese makers were becoming less in number, their production methods and numbers of overall cheese manufactured were constantly rising, though still not on the scale of the much larger factory creamery producers; as John Green recalled, "The number of farmhouse makers were dropping fast, but the Milk Marketing Board allowed for two or more farmers to co- operate together, taking milk from the neighbouring farms, and in so doing the gallonage increased."

As these remaining farmhouse cheese makers declined, many people seriously wondered about the whole future of farmhouse cheese making, which had survived so many ups and downs for nearly a thousand years.

For myself being introduced to cutting and packing at Crump Way, I have seen how vastly the type of 'Cathedral City', the flagship brand was not only to change, but also be part of the major changes coming into the industry.

It was by way of setting up the cheese samples for the daily grading sessions, that, I got introduced into the art of cheese grading and judging of cheeses at agriculture shows.

The key people at Crump Way in my time there were Stan Thorp, Gordon Walker and Philip Thorp, who looked after the management of the company and the cheese sales, while it was Bill Howe and John Plenty that got me introduced to cheese grading.

Double Devon Delights! Elise and Gary Jungheim at the Tavistock Cheese Fair 2013.

Looking back, it is now as ever a serious exercise, assessing a cheese sample, by that we mean a whole cheddar cheese being one taken from a whole vat, which could range from 20 to 60 made per vat, and depending on how many vats were made during a month's production, each grading session could be 30 up to 100 plus cheddars to be tried and recorded.

The legal grading period was to be for 3 months of age, though over the years, cheese can be assessed at 1 month of age, and also 6 months of age, and these sessions are before those of the commercial gradings and tastings for the customers such as the supermarkets who often bring their own cheese grader or technologist.

"A good sense of smell is a priority if anyone wishes to be a cheese grader", is what I often remark to people enquiring about assessments of cheese, whether it is to the public at agriculture and trade shows or at cheese grading courses I have helped to tutor.

The overall aim of the initial cheese grading, is to find not only the keeping qualities of each individual vat of cheese, and how you expect the cheese to mature to such an age, bearing in mind, the legal requirement for mature cheese must be from 9 months and over; while at the same time looking out for any problems in the cheese which can result from many factors, what the cows ate, the quality of the milk and any problems in the manufacture.

For the grading sessions, there is one or sometimes two graders along with the farmer and his cheese maker to discuss the merits of each individual cheese sample. A points system ranging from the good long keeping to the lesser quality is recorded and signed off at the end of each grading and an appointment made for the next month's grading session.

The more in depth you go with the cheese grading, you can ascertain some cheeses that may well be worth a second look at, for the purposes of entering agricultural and trade cheese shows, along with the knowledge what each individual customer is looking for, which makes the gradings even more interesting.

Though this is often the case, even when there are problems, it is trying to find the source of any irregularities than can also be rewarding.

It certainly keeps you awake and aware what is going in; though having said that, there was once one occasion when a certain cheese maker arrived for the afternoon grading session, and being an already long day for him, he proceeded to sit down, and in this case he led down in the centre of the grading room on a trolley and quickly went to sleep, whereupon I asked my colleague John Plenty, "Shall we wake him up?" John replying, "Will you?" Anyway, we finished the grading, and as we did, the cheese maker awoke, and asked "Everything alright?" and quickly signed the Cheese Grading Certificate and went back to the farm for another long session. Probably the first time I have sent anyone to sleep, a priceless moment!

While constantly adapting to continual changes within the market place, another major blow for all farmers, including those not manufacturing their milk, was to come with the discontinuing of the 'monthly milk cheque', though to help compensate farms selling cheese through the Milk Marketing Board, the then owned processing arm of the board, Dairy Crest, gave "favourable financial terms" to some cheese makers, while others would have to finance themselves.

John Green recalls these times and other contributing factors, "Around this time there were only 9 farmhouse cheese makers still producing 60 pound (30 kilos) round wrapped cloth cheese, the remainder had switched over to 40 pound (20 kilos) sealed block production."

"At that time, we collected milk from 5 local farms, and our peak intake was 2,700 gallons (14,000 litres) of milk daily, which was around

600,000 to 700,000 gallons (3,000,000 to 3,500,000 litres) annually" added John.

I recall my first visit to Thames Ditton, the head office of the Milk Marketing Board during this period, which was situated close to Surbiton and even had its own railway branch line!

What I remember so well, was the sheer number of people working there, as this was pre our technological age of today, for seeing a mass of tall computer banks with spinning wheels of data, like something out a science fiction film, and for me to be introduced directly to Detta O'Cathain, the Managing Director (later to become Baroness Detta O'Cathain) on my first visit, raised a few heads, as to who is this person from Somerset!

It was also to be a period of time when the words 'rationalisation' and 'deregulation' were to become more apparent in the whole dairy industry, and my first visit, would be not only the start of several visits to other Milk Marketing Board locations, but seeing and being part of the major changes soon to take over the industry.

By 1983, 70% of the country's cheese, including that of farmhouse cheddar, was now in the block shape format, and the once 8 internal sections of cold stores of the wholly 'traditional' Crump Way premises in Wells, was a fifty – fifty ratio and increasing towards a 'block' store warehouse, culminating in around 1,500 forty pound (20 kilos) cheeses per row, at 40 rows per store!

In 1984, as a result with discussions with the Milk Marketing Board, Coombe Farm Holdings of Crewkerne, Crump Way of Wells and Whitelocks Ltd of Whitchurch in Shropshire, merged together as Mendip Foods, under the chairmanship of Simon Oliver, with the aim to develop and improve sales of farmhouse cheese, and to compliment, their new state of the art 'packing unit' premises at nearby Frome, to the east of Wells.

While today's terminology uses such phrases as 'global marketing', Mendip Foods, very quickly went on to become one of Britain's top three suppliers of cheese, having at that period of time, around 20% share of the market place.

Very quickly, Mendip Foods at Frome and Wells became part of the mighty Dairy Crest, with them having the key brand 'Cathedral City', which by now was a different tasting cheese with more consistency, and among the other brands was the seemingly appropriate 'Joseph Harding' used for 'vintage reserve cheddar', named after the leading cheddar pioneer from the local area.

For the cheese makers that had been supplying Crump Way, a few saw 'deregulation' as a point to being bold and make an independent stance, such as Alvis Brothers of Redhill, just to the south of Bristol, Ashley Chase near Dorchester in Dorset, A.J. and R.G.Barber of Ditcheat, North Bradon at Isle Brewers near Taunton, Tower Farms of Lydeard St. Lawrence also near Taunton and T.W.Clothier of Bruton.

The winds of change in the dairy industry, came to a harsh reality in October 1987, when what was to be an almighty hurricane swept across the southern counties, and also caused damage. to the offices of Mendip Foods Commodity Trading, literally taking the roof of the building and crashing into the cars below, and not even a wind break with lorries and trailers set into position could help defect the strong winds.

Time does not stand still, and sadly for Wells, its last links with the cheese industry was the winding down to the final closure of Mendip Foods Commodity Trading, being the former Crump Way store , for Dairy Crest now had the market leader 'Cathedral City' at its brand new premises at Frome, while for Wells, the site was a shadow of its former self, and for the remaining cheese makers , mostly the cylindrical shape, 'traditional' members, where would the cheese be stored now, were just one of the endless list of questions being asked?

In fact, it was to be another hurdle the cheese makers such as the Green family had to overcome, and in their plans for the future, they made a major investment in building a new cheese dairy, about a half a mile away from their original dairy in the village of West Pennard.

It was as though history was repeating itself, and for various reasons, the circle had come around again, and the family and all the other remaining cheddar makers had to start selling their cheese themselves to the market place, and the future of these remaining businesses will be profiled in a later chapter.

CHEESE MAKING IN SOMERSET

Whether it is just one of the many myths of Somerset, and in particular relating to the fabled folklore around the Glastonbury area is in fact still open to question, and concerns tales of the Monks of Glastonbury Abbey, whom stored milk in their leather pouches.

It was apparently on one such occasion that during a storm in the weather, the Monks travelling through Cheddar Gorge, took shelter in one of the numerous caves; whereupon they discovered the milk had curdled into a curd formation, with the 'cheese' being named, Cheddar, after the name of the village.

There are many different versions of this 'tale', and this account seems the more plausible, though one fact that has remained, is the constant temperature and humidity inside the caverns, which are ideal for the storing and maturing of cheddar cheese, and again whether this fact was originally known at the time of the Monks of Glastonbury is still open for debate.

Who would have thought, that in our technological age, traditional cheddar cheese would be stored in the other famous caves of Somerset's Mendip Hills at Wookey Hole near Wells, in the 21st century; proving what comes around goes around!

Up in Yorkshire, it can be conclusively proven that the Monks of Jervaulx Abbey, had a recipe for making cheese, whom even Miss K.D.Maddever, has cited, "Dare one suggest that Glastonbury Abbey may have left recipes from which evolved the famous Cheddar cheese of Somerset?"

Life tends to be a little confusing in Somerset, bearing in mind the central Cheddar cheese making area, known to all born and bred locals, is part of the 'Moors', a paradox of meaning to today's branded image of the 'Somerset Levels'; for the low lying land, much of which is below sea level, is in stark contrast to the hilly counterparts of the same name, found in Yorkshire.

It is on the 'Moors' and along the edge of the nearby Mendip Hills, which themselves rise up to over 1,000 feet above sea level are such a contrast of contours for the cheese making area, matched only by the Cheshire cheese makers with their area of manufacture being similar in landscape and is known as the 'Cheshire Plain'.

Somerset, along with its other heritage of Cider making, make this

Cheddar cheese, two main ingredients for its trade and tourism; an aspect raised as early in 1794, when the then form of agriculture department remarked, 'The main cheddar making area is Axbridge, Cheddar, Glastonbury and Shepton Mallet'.

South of the county, the report goes on to add, 'It is mainly butter making', while going further south westerly into Devon and Cornwall, the article states 'they are widely known for butter and cream' adding 'little attention was paid to cheese'.

Over 200 years on into the present, while both Devon and Cornwall are without doubt the leading 'cream tea' counties, (I am not going to get drawn into which is the proper way of putting the jam and cream on the scones, which always causes much debate, but to say they are both lovely to eat!) Both counties have however now become major suppliers of Cheddar cheese and have had an integral effect on the small farmhouse cheese makers of Somerset, due to the monolithic monsters of Cornwall's Davidstow and Devon's Taw Valley creamery factories.

Today, looking back to find some point of time as a possible commencement for Cheddar, is made even harder, by the fact at the time of writing just over 10 farmhouse cheddar makers are left, and when I made the first draft of this book in 1999, there were 23 such cheese makers remaining!

Out of these only two reside in Devon, with even the seemingly invincible Denhay Farms near Bridport in Dorset, causing the biggest shock in 2013, by ceasing cheese production, a factor based on financial returns being unsatisfactory and loss-making, factors that also affected three other local cheese makers to either shut down their businesses or to find other ways to survive the bleak, economical, times of this period.

Of today's remaining farmhouse cheese makers, three of them can trace their farming histories back into the 1500's, but whether they were actually making farm made cheddars is still open for final conclusion.

As time went on, evidence of the craft is more reliable, and are joined in the 1800's by the Longman family of South Somerset, and later reaching the 1900's by such names as the Clothier family of Bruton, the Keen family from Wincanton, the Saunders family on the Mendip Hills and the Green family of West Pennard, were all becoming well, known names in the farmhouse cheese making of Somerset Cheddar.

The first precise description of 'Cheddar' was recorded in 1856, seventeen years after the famous 'Great Pennard Cheese', when there was an enquiry into the methods of cheese making in the county, as well as neighbouring Gloucestershire and Wiltshire, with the report, being published, in the Bath and West Journal of 1857.

It was during this period of time, the likes of Joseph Harding were having a major influence on the new methods of making cheddar cheese; and also being an educationalist, Harding was the first to enquire about the creating of 'Dairy Colleges', which would help improve the quality and get a form of consistency which was lacking amongst the then cheese makers of the era.

Cutting the replica West Pennard Cheddar overlooked by cheese maker David Higdon and John Green, with the author helping too.

Among the other pioneers, in radically changing the course of events in the evolution of Somerset cheese making were a Mr. T.C.Candy who originated from across the border in Cattistock in Dorset, whom was to introduce the 'Candy system', which included among its principal recipes, that the cheese was to be made with a high scald factor temperature.

A third notable person, to help bring some form of unity to the industry of the time, was Henry Cannon, whom was to be more of a genuine local pioneer, for he not only came from Milton Clevedon near

Evercreech, but he was to be responsible for the meticulous approach to cheese manufacture with much attention to detail, emphasising the importance of the cleanliness of its principal ingredient, the milk.

With nearby Wells, having as already stated, the very first 'Cheese School', Henry Cannon's daughter, was to be appointed the Bath and West Society Cheese School teacher.

One long lasting aspect of the 'Cannon system', which the author was very privileged to see and assist in the actual cheese making, was to be the very unique way of pressing the 'cheddared curd', which was piled on top of wooden racks (*This was pre health and safety days I can assure you!*), within a small open 'cooler', with the curd wrapped around within a large muslin cloth, whereupon another wooden rack was placed on top again, being held down by several weights!

Keeping my own records of this occasion, of which I'm sure Henry Cannon may well of approved, dates back to Thursday 27th March, 1986, during a visit to one of Somerset's last remaining unpasteurised farmhouse cheddar cheese makers, being the Keen family, whom farm at Moorhayes Farm in Charlton Musgrove, near Wincanton.

The farm was then under Mrs Dorothy Keen, and her two sons George and Stephen, and was at the time probably the very last, still making cheese in a square ended tinned copper cheese vat, and also inside the actual farmhouse, hence the origins of farm made Cheddar.

Jack Parsons, was the then cheese maker at Keen's, and a couple of quotes from my report of the time, bear testimony to the ethics of Henry Cannon.

"The cheese maker here had previously worked for some of the older cheese making concerns, such as Rood, Tucker and Windsor, and has been at Keens for nearly twenty years'.

"It was to be the 'pitching', that I was to be amazed at, with its such hard manual intensive procedures, yet being so immaculate, precise and certainly methodical."

Back to the late 1800's, and in particular to the village of West Pennard, lying just a mile or so away to the east of the much fabled town of Glastonbury, the small hamlet is renown, for its place in Somerset farmhouse Cheddar history, more so for the Green family, who have been making the handmade cylindrical cheeses for several generations since the early 1900's; but the village is also known for an earlier cheddar cheese, but of much larger proportions, going on to have a place in local folklore as the 'Great Pennard Cheese'.

So for the next few pages, it is well worth documenting the origins of this huge cheese, which actually dates back to 1839, and typically there is much to distinguish between fact and fiction.

As one of the local papers, the 'Wells Journal' and its sister periodicals, the 'Somerset and West of England Advertiser' and the 'Frome, Shepton Mallet, Glastonbury and Axbridge Gazette' did not come into print until 1851 onwards, there is very little local documented evidence.

Even the nearby village of Cheddar, and its Parish Records, make only a fleeting retrospection.

In fact, it is the Dorset paper, that reports of its making, being ascertained from the 'Sherborne Journal' of 1839.

So what was so newsworthy about a cheese at this point in time? The answer seems to go back a year or so earlier to Queen Victoria's accession to the throne in 1837, when during one of those years, Queen Victoria was apparently presented with a large loaf of bread.

With this gesture in mind and a seemingly talking point for the farmers of West Pennard and some of the neighbouring hamlets of East Street, Woodland Street and Sticklinch, they were to agree amongst themselves, that bread seemed a poor relation without its stable ingredient – cheese!

To make the gesture even more noteworthy, as something really patriotically consented and agreed by the group of farmers, they all decided to give a whole days milk into making one special cheese, and with so much milk, it was also agreed to make one 'big' cheese, that had never been made before, adding to the uniqueness of the planned gift to the Queen.

The 'Sherborne Journal' gave amongst the named people of the time, as John Wright, who worked as a blacksmith in Glastonbury, who made the special 'press' for the cheese, quoting, "John Wright, has made, and very recently, no less than 90 presses", though this was to be a larger piece of machinery, likewise is said for the 'vat', the cheese mould, which is quoted as , "being octagonal, measuring three feet in diameter, and made by Joseph Smart of Glastonbury, concluding "the principal part of the machinery was made by George Naish of West Pennard."

The 'Sherborne Journal' concludes with, "In the making of the Royal cheese, every transaction from beginning to end was conducted in the most orderly manner and every department was efficiently superintended by William Norris, aided by his friends."

It was on the morning of June 28th, 1839, that the 'Great Pennard Cheese' was made, with the milk coming from over 700 cows donated by the local farmers, having seven of the largest cheese tubs in West Pennard also being borrowed for the day; with the production being undertaken by no less than 26 dairymaids.

Somehow, the sheer hard work by the dairymaids seems to have been forgotten, for as part of the ongoing celebrations, a song was composed by a Mr.T.Dibdin, being set to the music by Mr. T.Williams

'The Pennard men then built a cheese,
The like was never seen!'
'Twas made and pressed, and fit to please,
Our gracious lady Queen!'
'And wedded to her royal love,
May blessings on her fall'
'And Pennard cheese at dinner prove,
The best thing – after all!'

According to the 'Sherborne Journal', "during the time of making, little or no difficulty presented itself."

Making a special top for the cheese, or better known as a 'cheese follower', a term still used today, this was to be in the hands of a craftsman from Wells, named William Halliday, who was to create the Royal coat of arms for Queen Victoria onto a huge wooden, cheese mould follower.

The original follower was about 3 inches thick of solid mahogany wood, and was octagonal in shape and fitted onto the top of the cheese during pressing, with the intention that the coat of arms would then appear embossed on the top of the huge cheese.

As well as the cheese going on to have a turbulent life, the 'cheese follower' was also, to have a documented life ,as we shall soon discover!

If the actual day's production had been eventful, starting off with the local bells ringing and firing of a cannon at about 5am in the morning, the day would later conclude with a dinner being held at the 'West Pennard Inn', being provided by Mr and Mrs Court, with William Norris presiding over the loyal and patriotic toasts.

After the cheese had been pressed and removed from its large mould, the unique octagonal shaped cheese would finally give its renown statistics of being a weight of about half a ton, or over 500 kilos, with the circumference of 9 feet or 2.7 metres, along with a diameter of 37 inches or 92.5 centimetres and a height of 22 inches or 55 centimetres.

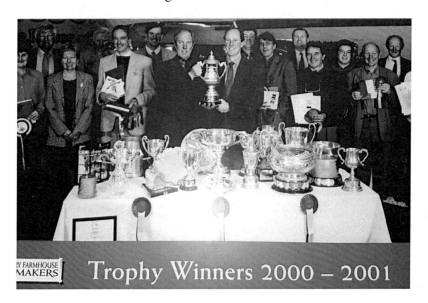

Trophy Winners 2000 – 2001

Glory Days: Members of the West Country Farmhouse Cheesemakers in celebratory mood at their head office.

Despite these impressive facts, the cheese was to have a few technical problems, which was not surprising, mainly due to the mahogany wood 'cheese follower' becoming stuck, and had to be taken apart in sections.

According to the 'Sherborne Journal', of October 3rd, 1839, the huge cheese during the week commencing September 23rd for the next five days, between the hours of 11.30am and 2.00pm, it "was open for public inspection", and in so doing, "No public exhibition in town or country has lately produced a greater influx of company in countless numbers."

Such was the demand to see this creation, that during the month of October, the cheese would be on display every Tuesday and Thursday from 11.30am until 3.00pm, with a manager appointed to look after its safe keeping along with answering the varied questions.

According to a much later source, of 90 years on, the 'Somerset

Year Book' of 1928, had the very first constructive article written about the 'Great Pennard Cheese', recalling the following month of November 1839, "the cheese was stated to be progressing to maturity with every prospect of ultimate success", going on to add, "It had that week been conveyed by the manual assistance of 16 able-bodied mechanics to a place of greater convenience", being the premises of John Dunkerton.

By now, other notable publications were making reference to the publicity the cheese was creating, including the 'London Globe', citing "Her majesty and ministers would find the cheese, never exceeded in quality."

According to the Somerset Year Book, this quote caused a bit of a stir with some of the west country publications, such as the 'Woolmer's Exeter' and 'Plymouth Gazette', feeling there was some form of political interference over the publicity it was creating, stating, "Her majesty's ministers are it appears, ex-officio majesty's cheese tasters."

The following year, on the Queen's wedding day of February 10th, 1840, more celebrations were to occur in the village of West Pennard, for the cheese was now pronounced to be almost ripe, confirmed by its 'promoters' William Norris and John Dunkerton.

By Whitsun, the cheese was continuing to mature well, and equally to keep public interest in its ageing and related publicity, so much so that after the church service in West Pennard, it is also reported by the Somerset Year Book, that "little short of a thousand persons were liberally enabled by John Dunkerton, to drink her majesty's health with the respective bands playing the national anthem."

The celebrations seemed to be going on an eternity, particularly among the local farmers, whereupon one occasion, the county's other renown asset 'cider' was very popular, and it was stated, "from twenty to thirty hogsheads of cider disappeared down the throats before the cheese was 'ripe'."

Finally the 'Great Pennard Cheese' was taken to London by a delegation of farmers from West Pennard, as well as from the small hamlets of East Street, Sticklinch and Woodland Street.

It was reported that Queen Victoria, preferred a more mature cheese, whether that was by way of a stronger flavour, or by its actual age, but all was not lost, for she deemed that it be presented again at a future date; the farmers announcing very quickly, they would return the cheese for the Royal Christening!."

The Somerset Year Book of 1928, cites of the triumphant return to Somerset, with a tongue in cheek humour, "Her majesty was very kind to the loyal farmers, who became known as the Marquis of Sticklinch, the Duke of Woodland, and Lord East Street!."

Apart from some slight early political interference, the 'Great Pennard Cheese' had been the cause of much interest and celebration for about a year or so, and certainly put the village on the map of Somerset, and also into much press coverage locally and nationally.

As with all good intentions, there were alas, others who were not so enamoured by all its success, and there were reports, according to the Somerset Year Book, that, "Attempts were made to seize it or to damage it, and it is stated that an iron cage had been made for its safe custody", though in reality, the report goes on to add, "this may have been intended as a protection from vermin."

There was however an opposition by a rival group to actually cause damage to the cheese, and in so doing managed to get hold of the cheese vat and its wooden 'cheese follower', and made a plaster cast of the famous cheddar, taking it to London and even exhibited the imitation with a degree of much success!

Not to be outdone, the farmers were quick to get the genuine 'Great Pennard Cheese' on display in London as being the authentic original, presented at the Egyptian Hall, in London's Piccadilly.

The opposition were equally well organised, and managed to get an injunction served on the real farmers, prohibiting their exhibition!

Sadly, for the farmers, they had to legally fight their corner in the Courts, dampening what was to be a major celebration; but thankfully common sense, seems to have won the day, with the then Lord Chancellor dissolving the injunction in the real farmers favour.

Though their presentation in London had been marred by such counterfeiting, the farmers had won their case, and the resulting news coverage was also to be in their favour; so much so, the 'Great Pennard Cheese' returned home once more to its home county of Somerset, and then preceded to go on an exhibition tour of the county's largest towns.

Whether or not the original cheese vat and 'cheese follower' were ever returned is not known for sure, though it was widely reported, copies of the 'cheese follower' were indeed made for the real farmers, most of whom who were involved in its manufacture.

With all this sudden glory, the farmers involved, had become overcome by its continuing success, and instead of investing the revenue they were getting, it is noted in the Somerset Year Book, "Instead of taking care of the admission fees, spent them freely and were several hundreds of pounds out of pocket besides" and as a small consolation, "The opposition party were also losers by the law and other expenses to about an equal amount."

The final period of time of the huge cheese life, is also very vague in its reported history, though it is known it was in the Sticklinch area of West Pennard, until the death of the farmer there, whereupon it was moved to another of the village's hamlets of Woodland Street, where it is quoted in the Somerset Year Book, "It was then removed to Woodland, where it rested, an unfortunate, worn-out, neglected giant, until the 'Duke' gave up farming, and took upon himself the management of the 'Old Down Inn' on the Mendip Hills.

The 'Old Down Inn' still survives to this day, being part of the village of Emborough, a few miles to the north of Wells, and interestingly, just the short distance away from the premises of another former farmhouse cheese maker, being that of the Saunders family, who up to their ceasing (of) production had made cheese for three generations themselves, and by way of some coincidence, the Saunders family also started out in business under the shadow of the Glastonbury Tor, on the lanes around West Pennard and Brindham!

The only sure fact, and really disappointing truth, despite one brief visit to Queen Victoria, due to the legal battles in the Courts; the huge cheese, was never finally received by her majesty Queen Victoria.

Worst still, if the report in the Somerset Year Book of 1928 is indeed accurate, then the ultimate fate is recorded as, "It went the way of all giants, leviathans, mammoths, and nine day wonders. Let us draw a veil over its wretched ending: it was given to the pigs."

With the best of such endeavours, it is a pity that such reports were to be very scarce, over what was really a significant part of the history and heritage of Somerset, and one of its important traditions, being that of cheddar cheese making.

It would be another 150 years before there would be a chance to recreate this unique piece of Somerset folklore, of which the Green family cheese makers of West Pennard would be involved, and to a lesser degree the author, who had to help 'grade' the second 'Great Pennard Cheese'.

If indeed the first celebratory cheese did end up being fed to the pigs, what can be added about the farmers and the machinery?

According to the 'Castle Cary Visitor', a publication of August 1908, it quotes the 'cheese follower' with its coat of arms was still "in the possession of James Naish, a butcher at West Pennard", going on to add appropriately, "May we hope that it will find its way in time to the Somerset County Museum, there to be preserved both as a work of art, and as a relic of one of the most amazing village enterprises on record."

As it has already been stated, there were 'allegedly' many copies of the 'cheese follower' made, and this was born out by the 1928 photograph in the Somerset Year Book, differing slightly from the 1989 photograph in the Somerset and Avon Life magazine, with the former being discovered at Burnham on Sea on the Somerset coast, while the latter comes from Stoke St. Gregory near Taunton; still at least, neither had left the county, and continues in part to make the story ever more intriguing.

It was in the late 1800's, and the Bath and West Society's strong links to all aspects of agriculture, that is was a period in time when people were looking into the problems related to cheese making and asked Dr F.J.Lloyd in 1891 to make some research, concluding "It became evident that the science of cheese making had to deal not merely with chemical questions, but also to a large extent with bacteriological questions", with Dr F.J.Lloyd also inventing the acidimeter using titration.

If improvements and a radical overall of the county's cheese making was slowly and surely being implemented, the sales and production of farmhouse cheddar had not diminished, with prices rising from 66 shillings per hundredweight and steadily climbing in value each year.

In the mid central area of Somerset, it was Messrs Hill Brothers of Evercreech who were to become the principal cheese factors, whom visited nearby farms, making an assessment of the quality of the months production and making an offer for the product, and as Miss.K.D.Maddever rightly recalls, "Much haggling took place."

Lying directly westwards, and uniquely linked by the Burnham on Sea branch line of the Somerset and Dorset Joint Railway; Evercreech Junction was not only at the heart of the farmhouse cheddar cheese making, with A.J.and R.G.Barber of Dicheat, which was literally just down the road and nearby, neighbours T.W.Clothier were at Bruton, while eastwards along the line at Charlton Musgrove, the Keen family had the historic rail route go straight through their farmland and to the west H.G.Green of West Pennard also had the line very close by.

The Somerset and Dorset branch line, took the cheeses to Highbridge and its market, whose cheese sales had now increased in tonnage, taking over from the Wells Market which was left to the selling of livestock. The selling of the farmhouse cheddars at Highbridge were often conducted on the ground.

While there was much cheddar, it was in fact, Caerphilly that was still the main cheese being up for sale there, with the quick ripening cheeses still being sold mainly to South Wales.

W.H.Palmer and Sons were the auctioneers at Highbridge, and during the peak years of their business, which was always held weekly on Tuesdays, between 50 and 100 tons of Caerphilly were regularly put for sale under the gavel, and while for these smaller cheeses were in general very regular in size and weight, it was the dimensions that were still a cause of problem with the cheddars, which ranged from 15 pound up to 70 pound, and still some over one hundredweight!

As said, this was also the era, that some of the county's principal cheese making familes were making their names known to a wider clientele, such as T.W.Clothier starting out in 1861, at Wyke Champflower, very close to Bruton, and while today it is probably the largest farmhouse cheesemaker, the family still hold their roots to the core of the business, always referring to founder Ivy Clothier and her recipe of cheese making, seeing the business move from the in house copper vat cheese making and round cheeses over to the more convenient block cheese, which were held together by wrapping in a wooden box and lid, while they also used as time went on strong plastic containers.

By the early 2000's, the monthly tonnage had risen to 800 tons of cheese, with the main core brand being the 'Wyke', named after the small hamlet, and along with the cheddar, they like others to survive in the dairy industry, diversified into a range of cheeses, and also to prove very popular their brands, of salted and whey butter.

With the end of the former Milk Marketing Board, Crump Way closed, Wyke and all the others, also created their own pre pack units for their dairy products, with Wyke having theirs at nearby Wincanton, strategically close to today's A303; itself born out of the old trading routes to London.

Close by, a mile or so away to the west, Somerset's other large farmhouse cheddar cheese maker also started out in the 1800's, at the village of Ditcheat, the family firm of A.J. and R.G.Barber whose cheese making is a major employer in the area. Ditcheat also put on the map in recent years with the horse riding stables of the often champion trainer Paul Nicholls, with some horses owned by Paul Barber, of the family firm of A.J. and R.G.Barber whose cheese making is a major employer in the area.

Also at the start of the 2000's, the Barber family were producing 600 tonnes of cheese a month, with their main brands they were to build up over the years being 'Haystack' and 'Maryland', the latter named after their Maryland Farm along with their successful 1833 brand.

One key area, the public are not aware of, is that the family firm, even have a laboratory, making 'starter' which in the simplest of terms, is a key ingredient in the making of cheese, being a friendly bacteria, which is added to the milk, at the very start of cheese making, and will assist to give the cheese its distinct flavour, and while many versions are available, what may be appropriate and workable for some cheese makers, the same may not work for other cheese makers!

Also in the area, just to the south at North Cadbury, another long serving cheese making family of the Longman dynasty were to be founded in the early 1900's, and like the Barbers and Clothiers, were to change from cylindrical manufacture to block shape cheddar cheese production as time went on, with William Longman, the founder of the business creating his style of farm made cheddars, and if we keep to the bench mark of production by the early 2000's, theirs was to be 40 tonnes per month, and were to find a home for the health growing conscious with their 'Reduced Fat Cheddar' becoming very popular, while at the time of writing their 'Vale of Camelot' cheddar brand was making positive inroads into the dairy world.

Richard Longman's son and daughter now run the business, being Julius and Sarai Longman, with the latter diversifying into a sizable 'Cheese Sales' operation, selling a whole range of British and European dairy products.

To the north of the county, another of the well, known cheese families are the Alvis who come from Redhill, just to the south of Bristol and the nearby airport. It is their 'Lye Cross' brand of dairy products, named after their Lye Cross Farm, who have been manufacturing cheddar cheese for over 100 years, and by the early 2000's were up to 200 tonnes a month, though here it was to be their popular 'Organic' cheeses were to be their key brands.

So with the deregulation and rationalisation of the dairy industry since the ending of the Milk Marketing Board, the likes of the Alvis, Barber, Clothier and Longman families are just a glimpse of how these and Somerset's other remaining cheddar cheese makers have shown the way to adapt to constant changes in the industry.

While the Milk Marketing Board, was changing firstly into Milk Marque and quickly followed by being broken into three large co-operatives, it was just not the cheese making farmers who had to change with the times, it was also many of the antiquated factory creameries that either were lucky to expand and modernise while others, such as Yeovil's Dairy Crest's Watercombe and Sturminster Newton in Dorset, that were to close amongst many others including many milk bottling plants.

Evercreech, is one village dairy plant, which has often been the focus of many proposed closures over the years, it has somehow remained a major local employer, though the ownership of the old buildings would make a history book in itself, they have kept to a whole range of dairy products over the years, from cheese to yoghurts and even cream cakes.

The Somerset cheddar makers also had to get used to marketing and selling the cheese themselves, and while the West Country Farmhouse Cheese makers still survive the moving from Crump Way at Keward Farm in Wells, with a short period in Union Street in the city, they were to be finally based at the Royal Bath and West Showground.

Also out of the demise of the Milk Marketing Board, the British Cheese Board was formed, with former MMB Nigel White doing sterling work to help promote not just farmhouse cheddar, but the whole spectrum of British cheeses and has available a wide range of fact sheets dealing with all aspects related to cheese from health issues to recipes.

For the fate of the genuine cylindrical farm made cheddar cheese makers their future was not so rosy with the effects of the deregulation and rationalisation, with some sadly ceasing production altogether such as the Churchhouse family at Manor Farms in the actual centre of Castle Cary, J.K.Longman on top of Dicheat Hill,H.E and J.Grant of Trull near Taunton and even Chewton Dairy Farms owned by Viscount Chewton were to be casualties of the turbulent times.

One aspect, that is missed with these disappearing traditionalists is that they all had their own individual flavours, and I still recall the lovely firm yet smooth silky textures, and nutty flavours of the Grant cheddars, which were always of one size and shape, being slightly smaller at 25kg each; and more so visiting their farm, where it was one of the original part of the farmhouse productions.

The late Hughie Grant was one of those characters of the farming world, with his sons David and Graham taking on the small family business, while the original cheese maker Jack Cox retired it was here I first met Philip Rainbow, who was later to be part of a new era of artisan cheese making with the Somerset Cheese Company.

With changes within the industry, also came new faces, and a saviour for the unpasteurised cheese makers of the Keen and the Montgomery families was to be Randolph Hodgson, who had an artisan cheese business in London called Neals Yard Dairy, and was to be widely recognized for not only selling and promoting the cheese to a new clientele but equally gaining much positive press coverage and winning the hearts and minds of the new era of chefs all over Britain.

Part of the success was Randolph Hodgson who instigated the formation of the Specialist Cheese makers Association which the author has been a member since its formation back in 1989, and with the British Cheese Awards created by another key figure in the cheese trade, Juliet Harbutt, also coming out of the early Association Cheese Festivals, the first of which was at London's Butlers Wharf, Juliet, Randolph, and many other key people are to be credited for the renaissance of artisan cheese.

Also being on the Dairy Produce Committee of the Royal Bath and West Show, for twenty years, it was interesting to see a slow sea change of exhibits being entered, with the round cheddars being quickly outnumbered by the block versions at first, while slowly but surely different types of cheese were emerging and not just made with cow's milk, but from ewes, goats and buffalo as well!

Among the first of the new wave of artisan cheese makers were Mary Holbrooke and Frances Wood, with Mary coming from Sleight Farm at Timsbury near Bath, with the introduction of her fresh goats cheese called 'Tymsboro', while for Frances was to create a whole range of buffalo milk cheeses under such names as 'Junas' and 'Lambors' with her business situated at West Cranmore, near Shepton Mallet.

Also to follow on were the range of soft white cheeses from Graham Padfield, based at Park Farm, at Kelston near Bath, with the business known after his leading selling cheese 'Bath Soft Cheese', made from cow's milk.

For blue vein type of cheeses, Somerset was to join the ranks, with

Ian Arnetts, Exmoor Blue Cheese company, located at Willett Farm in Lydeard St Lawrence, near Taunton, with a diverse range of buffalo, cows, ewes and goats cheeses, with all having a blue vein and blue sounding names, such as 'Brendon Blue', 'Quantock Blue', 'Somerset Blue' an 'Willett Blue', amongst others.

Upholding the honour to be the last cheese maker in Somerset to be making Caerphilly, were R.A.Duckett and company of Walnut Tree Farm, in Wedmore. And is now made at Westcombe Farm.

Whitelake Cheeses from Bagborough Farm, Pylle near Shepton Mallet, under the auspices of Roger Longman, who had a short flirtation into making cheddar, created a whole range of goats cheeses with more success, with some delightful brand names such as 'Billy the Kid'!

Other emerging new cheese makers were to see Godminster Cheese at Bruton, producing a range of small waxed cheddar truckles, while near Wells, at North Wootton, the Bartlett brothers, James and David began introducing some jersey cow's milk cheeses and some unpasteurised ewe's milk cheeses.

Of all the new age of creative small cheese producers, the aptly named, Somerset Cheese Company, was born, being based in the former cheddar cheese dairy of John Longman, on top of Dicheat Hill, near Shepton Mallet, with one of the county's leading cheese makers Philip Rainbow, who had a CV working for the likes of the Grant and Saunders families, bringing to attention of the cheese world of whole new range of cheeses, such as 'Fosseway Fleece' made from ewes milk, 'Pendragon' created from buffalo milk, 'Pennard Ridge' being a goats milk style Caerphilly and the aptly titled 'Rainbow's Gold' made from Channel Islands milk.

Though these new names in the county of Somerset, poised no business threat to the cheddar makers, it was however just part of a major revival for small artisan cheese makers across Britain, with many factors coming together, such as the core foundations of the Specialist Cheese makers Association, the British Cheese Awards, new cheese dealers such as Randolph Hodgson and a growing range of food programmes on radio and television, supported by a new era of food writers such as Henrietta Green and Tamasin Day-Lewis, both of whom the author has had the privilege to judge with at the British Cheese Awards.

For the farmhouse cheddar cheese makers, those that were making the block shape versions were now competing with the large factory creameries, and to a degree, some traditional round cheddars were purchased by the supermarkets, the sales of such were not as they were, with the world economy showing signs of turbulence, there were winds of change in the cheese making world.

Given the emergence of the new breed of small artisan cheese makers in Somerset, even the large cheddar makers of Cricketer Farm, were to be taken over by Britain's largest goat business, of St Helen's Farm from Seaton Ross near York.

Even when, Greens of Glastonbury entered a goat's cheese at the Royal Bath and West Show, the fabled Juliet Harbutt, she declared when eventually finding out the name of the first prize winner, "Green's do not make goats cheeses!" (*Those who know Juliet, there were many expletives used*), but Greens had also now entered the new era of the diversity of cheeses.

Judges photocall including author at Mid Somerset Show 2014.

In fact, goats milk cheeses were being made in abundance in the county, with Lubborn Cheese, at Manor Farm, Cricket St. Thomas near Chard, creating with much success, brand names such as 'Capricorn' and 'Goats Brie', while their cow's milk soft cheeses of 'Somerset Brie' and 'Somerset Camembert' were of such quality they were on a par, and some would say better than the French counterparts, and having judged them over the years, the quality has been very consistent.

Given the boom years of the economy, the winds of recession finally blew into a major crisis, and with the supermarkets having such a dominance that after many years of lobbying evidence from Action for Market Towns, English Historic Towns Forum and the New Economics Foundation finally waking the Government up that there were serious issues to be addressed in the way we shop; and of such was to be just another factor facing the Somerset cheddar cheese makers.

With all the above factors, and also several years of poor weather, making animal feed extremely expensive, for the cows producing the milk, and along with spiralling costs of ingredients and packaging for the cheese, and more seriously bovine TB, even seeing whole herds of cattle being destroyed and cheese production either effected or sadly in the case of Brew Valley, the Clapp family, from Baltonsborough near Glastonbury giving up farmhouse cheddar cheese production altogether, it became very obvious that the county's once mighty 1,000 plus family concerns were now down to the last 10, and while the bigger enterprises will hopefully ride the storms, and the much smaller families have found their niche in the market place, let's hope they will all survive.

CHEESE MAKERS AND CHEESE SHOWS

As the new millennium continues, only 10 farmhouse cheddar cheese makers in the West Country survive, out of the post Second World War total of over 1,000 such family firms, with 7 left in Somerset and 2 in Devon and 1 in Dorset., with all of them now protected by the P.D.O., which is the Protected Designation of Origin, and still largely made by hand and to time honoured and traditional methods, handed down by the many generations of families.

Starting in Somerset, the big three we have already mentioned Alvis bros, Barber and Clothier families of Ditcheat and Wyke Champfower respectfully, and they hopefully have the strength to continue to compete with the factory creameries in their dealings with the major players, the supermarkets, though given all the contributing factors at the end of the last chapter, they also have good positive marketing and equally exporting skills, which have also got their names and that of Somerset on the world stage.

While by early 2000's standards some critics were questioning whether Barbers or Wyke are still farm related, with Barbers who were making around 600 tonnes of cheese a month equating to 7,200 tonnes a year and Wyke respectfully producing 800 tonnes a month or 9,600 tonnes a year, these figures are in fact still very small compared to the west country's pair of Davidstow and Taw Valley.

For Devon's Taw Valley factory creamery at this point of time were owned by Glanbia Foods followed eventually by Arla and Cornwall's Dairy Crest Davidstow were each manufacturing 2,500 tonnes a month or 30,000 tonnes a year, with a combined total of 60,000 tonnes; and this puts the production levels of Barbers and Wyke into perspective.

So with the closure of the once proclaimed 'Europe's largest cheese store' in Wells, there in keeping with a new era of regional distribution centres around Britain, massive warehouses were appearing on the landscape, which critics were calling 'sheds', and for Dairy Crest, their new distribution centre was to be based at Nuneaton in Warwickshire, with storage at this period of time being for 350,000 cheeses, being 100,000 more than the old Crump Way site in Wells.

So given all the circumstances of the ailing economy and the competiveness of the market place, Barbers and Wyke are doing sterling work for the county of Somerset in keeping farmhouse cheddar alive against the might of the factory creameries and all their marketing powers, more so as we will see, many of the once national companies were soon to be multi- national businesses making the farmhouse cheddar manufacture another challenge they will have to do business with rather than against.

Dorset's Ashley Chase at Parks Farm, located at Litton Cheney near Dorchester, have become part of the Barbers business, who at the dawn of the 2000's were making around 100 tonnes of cheese a month, and with Director Mike Pullin's expertise created the unique 'caved aged cheddar' a brand that has an image of going right back to the roots of Somerset's cheddar cheese history, and from its views of the world heritage site of the Jurassic coast, another growing brand of 'Coastal Cheddar' was born.

2012, was to be an exceptional year for Ashley Chase at the cheese and trade shows all over Britain, winning many 'Championships' including the International Cheese Show at Nantwich in Cheshire, with the author also helping to give, 'Caved Age Cheddar' the 'Best Cheddar Award' at the British Cheese Awards, proving if you can get a consistent product the rewards through shows but more importantly through sales help you immensely, in the fierce market place.

Its challenges like this, that are helping to keep farmhouse cheddar in the limelight, and the key for success, is to try and maintain a good position in the market place.

While, it is tragic Denhay Farms, no longer make their unique style of farm made cheddar cheese, it is however appropriate I give them a mention as a tribute to some of my recollections.

At the small hamlet of Broad Oak, just to the north of the bustling market town of Bridport, lies Dorset other well, known family firm of Streatfeild Hood, later to be widely known as Denhay Farms.

Yes it is not a spelling mistake, as Amanda Streatfeild, first told me, "The e comes before the, i." It was Commander Streatfeild, who began farming at Denhay Farm in 1952, in partnership with Lord Hood, having then around 300 acres, which by 1985 was to increase to about 1,750 acres, and having a herd of over 900 Friesian cows, with the business originally known as Streatfeild Hood and Company Limited.

By 1993, the company, now called Denhay Farms, had risen to just under 2,000 acres, with five herds of cows producing the milk to make their cheese.

I always remember one of their earlier cheese makers in Ken Corbin, later to be followed by William (Bill) Parsons, who was to be with the family business for over 30 years, and like all cheese makers, will tell you, getting up early, is all part of the job, to create cheddar cheese.

"It was not easy, even on my first day. I was told to start work at 6am, and turned up at 5.50am, to make a good impression, only to get a severe telling off, because there had been some misunderstanding, and I should have there at 5am!" recalls Bill in his humorous way.

Despite this setback, over the years Bill worked his way up the ranks to become head cheese maker, and such was the quality of his cheddar cheese, he won the prestigious Mendip Medal award for consistency of quality of cheese making at the Royal Bath and West Show, no less than 4 times between 1993 and 1998, not to mention two runner up spots, in all quite a remarkable record.

Having to help grade and later collate the results from all the other farmhouse cheese makers, was just another of my roles over the years in the farmhouse cheese industry.

Another fond recollection, was at the 1999 British Cheese Awards, at the Cadogan Hall, of the Duke of York's headquarters, in the Kings Road, London, when I was behind the trade stand, and we were having a blind tasting of tasting the difference between pasteurised and unpasteurised cheese, and using Denhay for the former and Keen's of Wincanton for the latter.

It was while one of the new era of food lovers, enjoying the cheese so much, she became very excited, passionately screaming "Yes! Yes! Yes! Yes!" recreating a scene from the film, 'Bob and Carol and Ted and Alice'. Needless to say, the bustling throng came to a sudden silence, with myself trying to keep a straight face, more so with Amanda Streatfield walking over to enquire if everything was alright, to which I replied "Yes", well what else could have I said! Another of those priceless moments.

Achieving high standards is seemingly all part of the business for Denhay Farms, for not only winning much silverware, trophies and prize cards at the country's leading agriculture and trade shows, another major part of the family business is their 'Denhay Pigs', the pride of George Streatfeild, who helped the firm win the 'Food From The Countryside' Award from the N.F.U. (National Farmers Union), for their dry cured bacon and unique air dried ham.

Amanda for a long period of time was the much respected Chairman of the Dairy Produce Section at the Royal Bath and West Show, while their manager Philip Crawford was to be for a period, the Chairman of the West Country Farmhouse Cheese makers, a role later taken on by George Streatfeild.

A fitting award for Amanda and George was to come at the British Cheese Awards of 2012, with them being merited the much deserved 'Cheese Persons of the Year', and it was a privilege to judge alongside them at the Devon County Show in 2013, just weeks before the announcement of the closure of the cheese making side of the business.

So while their cheddar cheese will slowly become nothing more than a memory, for being slightly dry, with a hazelnut flavour, their meat range will keep the Denhay farm flag flying.

If we follow the A35 from Ashley Chase and Denhay Farms in Dorset and head west into Devon, it is on the westerly outskirts of Exeter, we come to one of the two Devon cheddar cheese makers, with in the village of Newton St.Cyres is the location of Quickes Traditional Cheeses.

The family farm while dating back over 400 years, the history of cheese making goes back to Sir John Quicke and his wife Prue, who set up the cheese dairy, with today successfully run by Mary Quicke and while cloth bound cylindrical cheddars are the key product, they also make Double Gloucester and Red Leicester cheeses along with a popular hard goats cheese.

Like the recent demise of Denhay Farms, the Quickes also have a similar style of automated cheese racks that turn the cheese over, making for easier handling of the heavy cheeses.

While 'caved aged' cheddar has been a consistent marketing factor, Quickes have been fortunate to have had a great personality in Stuart Dowle, who has promoted the family cheese all over Britain, and is well known for his 'straw hat' as part of his character image, and at a recent International Cheese Show Awards at Nantwich in Cheshire, Stuart was richly deserved, the 'Cheese Personality of the Year'.

I have known Stuart for many years, and he is a credit to the cheese business, and I have always enjoyed the banter and working in his territory, either at the Devon County Show or the Real Cheese Fair in Tavistock.

While in Devon, we now travel, across the county up the A377 to the North Devon coast, and head towards the picture postcard fishing village of Clovelly, for not far away is one of the newer farmhouse cheddar makers of the Willes family, who are situated at Alminstone

Farm, who commenced production in 1984, and by the early 2000's were making around 200 tonnes of cheddar a month.

The business was set up by the late David Willes, with his son Peter who quickly rose up through the ranks as they say, while daughter Sarah looked after the administration.

David was a true workaholic, often commencing work at 3am to start cheese making, and would still have time to help run the farm, the myriad of meetings, and was also a Director of the British Cheese Board, and within five years of making cheese, they got the Reserve Champion Cheese at the 1999 Royal Bath and West Show, and were to go on to being one of the major suppliers for Pilgrims Choice, another fast growing cheese brand, the public were accepting.

Protecting the prizes as part of my stewarding duties at the Royal Bath and West Show, Shepton Mallet, Somerset in 1996.

Another major supplier into the Pilgrims Choice brand, as we return to Somerset, are the Baker family, who reside in the village of Haselbury Plucknett, which is between Crewkerne and Yeovil, to the south of the county.

It is at Leaze Farm, that the cheese making premises are situated in the heart of the 'Ham Stone' village, and at the early 2000's, they were making around 25 tonnes of block size cheddar a month, under the family of Brian and Christine Baker and their son Neil, with the cheesemaking undertaken by Philip Keys.

Such was their consistency of cheese manufacture, not only did they win the overall Championship at the Royal Bath and West Show in 1996, they also won the prestigious 'Mendip Medal' award for consistency of quality throughout 12 month periods, for both 1997 and 1998!

If they, were to be renown, for their cheese largely made by hand and to time honoured and traditional ways, the family also from time to time, gave over some of their fields to one of the county's well known outdoor events, being 'Yesterdays Farming', an event where you can glimpse an era where time has stood still, seeing other crafts such as 'hurdle making', 'thatching', 'threshing' and 'ploughing' taking place.

Alas, along with Brew Valley, Greens of Glastonbury, and Longmans were in 2012 and 2013, to be victims of the financial circumstances beleaguering the farming industry, and Bakers were also to stop cheese production.

It seems history seems to repeat itself, with the brand 'Cathedral City' originating out of the old Crump Way store in Wells, another growing cheese brand, that of 'Pilgrims Choice' has strong links to the Wells store and many of the supplying cheese makers.

It was North Downs Dairy, originating from Grove Dairy Farm, in Sittingbourne Kent; that built up the 'Pilgrims Choice' brand with their visits to the Wells cheese factors, and as the site went into shut down mode, they began purchasing the cheese direct from the various farms.

Such was the fast growing success of the brand, and making for economical, sense, North Downs also had their own cold stores and packing unit built close to the A303, in Wincanton.

As time went quickly on, and like 'Cathedral City', 'Pilgrims Choice' developed into a range of different flavour levels to suit customers tastes, and this growing trend coupled with the major changes within the dairy industry, with the companies becoming first by regional, then national and with it international, North Downs Dairy were to become part of Adams Foods, and so with the merger, the business of storing and packing moved to their head office in Leek in Staffordshire, and in turn were to become part of the Irish Dairy Board.

Moving over to West Somerset, under the shadow of the Quantock Hills and looking out over Bridgwater Bay, another of the county's long established cheese makers can be found.

It was after the Second World War, in 1948 that the press baron Lord Beaverbrook, started making farmhouse cheddar cheese at Stowey Court Farm, in what was then a large farm stable! And, it was William Jeanes four sons, and other local farmers who supplied the milk to make the cheese.

The name of the business, Cricket Malherbie, comes originally from one of the first farms Lord Beaverbrook bought, near Chard in South Somerset.

In 1978, Cricket Malherbie was then purchased by the Jeanes family, making largely farmhouse cheddar cheese, and with the ever changing market place and growing demands for other dairy products, the business branched out into both ewes and goats milk cheeses, along with butter and cream in their portfolio of dairy products.

With the busy A39 thoroughfare by passing the village of Nether Stowey, Cricket Malherbie soon established their farm shop and like Alvis Brothers at Redhill, they were amongst the pioneers in this form of marketing their products to the public in the form of farm shops.

The farm shop at Cricket Malherbie also has a 'viewing window' to watch the cheese making practices inside.

One aspect and in keeping to the roots of farmhouse cheddar cheese making and one of the unique customs of Somerset, is that the huge and weighty traditional farmhouse cheddar carried aloft in the colourful procession during the East Brent Harvest Home, is one made from Cricket Malherbie; and how proud the late Archdeacon Denison would be if he was alive today, being surely a fitting annual tribute to his memory, for fighting for the cause of West Country Farmhouse Cheddar.

Consistency as I have stressed throughout this book is a byword for the cheese makers, and Cricket Malherbie were not only to win the Championship Cheese at the 1998 Royal Bath and West Show, but equally the following year in 1999, being a very rare occurrence, and a tribute to the companies long serving brothers of Anthony and Richard Villis.

Time never stands still and during 1999, Cricket Malherbie were to be taken over by one of Britain's largest goat's milk products company of St.Helens Farm, from York.

The new owners were to be Angus and Kathleen Wielkopolski, having a controlling interest in the business, which in 1999, were making around 200 tons of goat's cheese, 1,000 tons of farmhouse cheddar cheese, and about 250 tons of other cow's milk cheese, mainly of the low fat type.

Across the Somerset Moors, on the old cheese trading routes to London, which has evolved into today's A30 Exeter to London thoroughfare, lies the market town of Crewkerne.

While Crewkerne still holds the ever popular 'St Batholomews Charter Fair', and while it is now purely of the pleasure type, it was at one time in its long history dating back to around 1270, it was for a period a very popular Cheese Trading Fair, being then hailed as 'the greatest in the county', toppling both Bridgwater and Wells, and mention of the most fabled White Down Fair not far away, noted for its livestock also had cheese as one of its commodities.

It is at the nestling Coombe Farm, on the Crewkerne to Chard road of the A30, that is the location of another former farmhouse cheddar cheese maker of the A.H.Warren Trust Limited.

It was back in 1942, when Andrew Henry Warren was assisted in setting up in farming by another of the county's much respected farming and cheese making families of W.H.Longman from North Cadbury, starting in a partnership of £100 capital.

Moving into farmhouse cheese making, the business prospered, and was incorporated into A.H.Warren (Coombe Farm) Ltd, in 1954.

From 1954 to 1980, further farms were purchased, and it was Mr Warrens wish, that when he passed away, a Trust would be constituted, and so in 1983, the Warren Trust was formed.

By the 1990's, the participating farms of the Warren Trust amounted to a total herd size of around 3,500 cows.

Block shape cheddar cheese, was to be their staple dairy product, though as the 1990's came to an end, the business moved into organic cheese production, along with fruit flavoured ice creams and yoghurts, that quickly became a growing success.

Unlike the remaining Somerset farmhouse cheddar cheese makers, Coombe Farm, as they are better known, diversified and constantly adapted to the every changing market conditions and this is part of their philosophy.

The firm work alongside Waitrose in a range of dairy products, and launched a range of dairy desserts in 2000, along with supplying Waitrose own label English cheddar cheese.

For the organic side of the business, Prince Charles 'Duchy' organic milk used Coombe Farm to pack their milk, and also that of Yeo Valley's organic milk; however in 2006, the cheese side of the business was to come to a close and by 2010 its milk operations were sold to Yeo Valley.

Mid Somerset Show Cheese Tent 1997

Despite the constant changes, it was a pleasure to grade and assess their cheese alongside the late William Birchenough who passed away in 1989 and his successor Martyn Gosney who went on to win the 1995 Championship Cheese at the Royal Bath and West Show.

Sadly with the passing away of Andrew Warren, William Birchenough and more recently the shock departure of Philip Cook, the long serving Nancy Ralphs (although, I always address her as Miss Ralphs as respect), was to be richly deserved the Chairmanship of the company, and when we used to have our post grading assessments, she always gave her glances with her eyes and ears, much in the vein of Miss K.D.Maddever.

Over on the Mendip Hills, just to the north of Wells, at the village of Emborough, was to be another farmhouse block size cheddar maker that, was on the scale of production as Coombe Farm, run in the latter years by Morgan Saunders.

The company statement quoted, 'Our commitment to quality and customer service is equalled by our desire to provide our customers with the cheese products that they need to succeed in today's marketplace'

While cheddar was their core product, like others in the dairy industry, the family moved into other different cheeses such as Colby and Monterey Jack, as well as low fat and reduced fat cheddars for the more health conscious.

They had two well known, cheese makers in the late Eric Hobbs snr, and his son of the same name Eric Hobbs jnr, while the firms later production manager had an aptly named cheese surname, being Christopher Stilton.

Sadly like that of Coombe Farm, they also stopped production, with the site eventually turning into a storage unit business, while Morgan moved into video production.

Back on the Somerset Moors, lies another of the county's last farmhouse cheddar cheese makers, at the village of Baltonsborough, lying in the shadow of the famous Glastonbury Tor, being the location of West Town House, where the Clapp family reside.

Before going into cheese production, the family were manufacturing that other fabled Somerset product, Farmhouse Cider, and it was in 1958 that they started making cheese under the late Bob Clapp snr, starting off with Caerphilly, and by 1960 they went into cylindrical cheddar production, which they maintained for around 25 years, before switching over to block shape cheddar, largely due to the demands of the marketplace conditions.

From 1958 to 1998, they were blessed in having an excellent cheese maker in William (Bill) Melhuish, who also taught family members Bob Clapp jnr and Simon Clapp, the unique art of farmhouse cheddar cheese making.

Though Bill Melhuish retired at the end of 1998, he went out in style, winning the highly acclaimed Mendip Medal awards at the Royal Bath and West Show for three years in a row of 1995 to 1997. Bill

Melhuish jnr, took over in his father's footsteps, working his way up from assistant cheesemaker to head cheesemaker.

R.L.Clapp and Sons, were to change their name to Brew Valley Farm, and unfortunately like so many in the dairy industry, were to struggle in getting a fair price for their cheese, coupled with that other scourge of the farming community, bovine TB, hit the family firm so much, that enough was enough, and hopefully their growing butter business will keep their name in the dairy trade, along with diversifying into a lucrative mozzarella cheese production.

Before I conclude, with what some critics and purists will say are the real last of the Somerset cheddar makers, I have mentioned some of the agriculture and trade shows, so now is an appropriate time to give a more in depth look in relation to the cheese makers.

Without doubt, the Royal Bath and West Show, is the West Country Farmhouse Cheese makers principal and premier shop window to the public.

The show season, for entering cheeses used to start at the North Somerset Show, being originally held on the bank holiday Whitsun Monday at the end of the month, when it was originally, held in the grounds of Ashton Court near Bristol.

The show itself dates back to 1856, and with the massive Royal Bath and West Show starting two days later on the Wednesday, it was the ever increasing demands of logistics, they saw there was a need for a major change, and despite early fears of a downturn in attendance, there was to be an actual increase in public support.

The North Somerset Show first moved to the other bank holiday of May Day on the first Monday of the month, with the venue still being the grounds of Ashton Court, and for nearby Bristolians, the event was just a short stroll over the city's famous landmark, the Clifton Suspension Bridge, spanning the river Avon and the scenic Avon Gorge, linking the city to the countryside.

Alas, there were to be a few years of poor weather, that saw a drop in attendance, and a newer site was to be found in the grounds of the National Trust's Tyntesfield just a mile or so away.

While there was a cheese and dairy section on the old site at Ashton Court, which the author has judged at, there are still no signs of the event being revived as yet, it is here that I had the privilege to judge alongside the late Arthur Hamilton, who resided out of nearby Backwell.

Following on from the North Somerset agriculture event, it is now the Devon County Show that really gets the cheese exhibiting under way.

Held as a three day event, of a duration of Thursday to Saturday in May, and a about a week before the Royal Bath and West Show, its origins date back to the Exhibition Fields in the Whipton area of Exeter, but as the show grew larger and ever more popular, a new permanent and larger site was finally found being the land of the Westpoint Exhibition Centre at Clyst St Mary, on the eastern outskirts of Exeter, and having in turn excellent road, rail, park and ride and even air facilities just a few minutes away, not to mention, even sea, if the tides or suitable, having pleasure boats navigating the nearby waters of the River Exe.

I have been invited many times to judge at the Devon County, and during the 1995, Centenary event, the author, also had the privilege to meet and demonstrate the art of cheese judging in the presence of her majesty the Queen, displaying the virtues of the then Champion Cheese, being Cheddar of course!

With Exeter, expanding in size of population to the east of the city, with a new village being created as Cranbrook, all adds to the vibrancy of the area where the showground is sited, and such is the popularity of the three day event thankfully it is still one of the few agriculture shows that remain loyal to its roots.

The Food Hall Tent is the location for the Cheese Show section, ably run by Sheila Ashford and her small team, and if we do not get our fill of cheese to taste, we are often awarded drinks and lovely cakes!

Like many cheese shows over the recent years, there has been an abundance of new cheeses made from various milks that make the display to the visitors even more colourful and pungent to smell.

While many of these new varieties are often as not, regional to this show, as others throughout the other cheese shows of Britain are likewise seldom to be found out of their areas, some however have made the next step in marketing.

I have been asked many times by the new era of cheese makers, on the ways forward, and I cite the small Somerset cheese producers of the Keen and Montgomery family, who have remained at their maximum capacity despite calls for major increases in production, and in turn have created their own niches in the market place.

While it is interesting to judge these new creations in the dairy industry, and I have in turn got used to the regional choices on offer around Britain, it is still tasting some of the newer ones that often make their debuts at the shows such as the Devon County even more intriguing as who and what they are and who made them, for as said all cheese show judging is undertaken blind with no clues to what they are, what they are made of and who made them!

When eventually after judging is complete and awards merited out, it is often the ones entered on behalf of local dealers or shop keepers, such as in the case of Country Cheeses of Tavistock, owned by Elise and Gary Jungheim, who debut other peoples hand-made cheeses. Elise and Gary have done much to promote the remaining cylindrical cheddar makers of Somerset in their shops in Devon, and as we will see, later on in these pages, they have also set up their own cheese event.

Along with the massive one day Nantwich and South Cheshire Show's International Cheese Show, the Royal Bath and West Show, are still considered the key cheese shows for entering exhibits.

If it is not enough of sheer hard work, determination and enthusiasm that goes into making farmhouse cheddar, the same goes on behind the scenes of the events, particularly with the Somerset event, which the author only knows too well, with twenty years served on the Dairy Produce Committee, as well as at the old Wells Crump Way site, preparing the traditional makers cylindrical cheddars for exhibiting!

From 1966 up to 1999, since the Royal Bath and West Show has been on its now permanent site, the members of the West Country Farmhouse Cheese makers were to win 29 Championships and 22 Reserve Championship awards in 34 years, making 51 out of a possible 68 trophies, surely a record never to be beaten!

The history of the large agriculture show dates back to 1777, and has been the subject of many a book; so it is just since it has been at the village of Prestleigh site, just south of Shepton Mallet, the spacious ground has also become the head office of the West Country Farmhouse Cheese makers after their final move from nearby Wells.

It was in 1964, that the contract for today's showground was signed, having the then 212 acre site being bought for £60,000 from farmer George Longman, and by the 1966 Show £100,000 had been spent on developing the site.

So what does go into entering a cylindrical cheddar for a show such as the Royal Bath and West, the answer is much hard work, as my days at the old Wells Crump Way site recall, for not only had I the privilege, but also much physical and mental determination to select the suitable exhibits.

To enter any show, the schedule rules must be adhered too, and equally the reading of the disqualification rules are a must, including whether the cheese should be tasted or not by using a cheese iron.

To get a cheese worthy of entering a cheese or trade show, this comes from the earlier cheese grading records and also the cheese maker's record book of manufacture, where early assessments have been made.

Four key points are continually assessed making the suitable credentials, for judging, with firstly, that of flavour and aroma, the body and texture, the colour of the curd and the finish and appearance.

Once the cheese has got all the right qualifications of age for its appropriate class of entry, the next stage is the final preparation and where the hard physical attributes come into use.

Firstly, each traditional cloth bound cheddar, has it outer muslin cloths taken off, to reveal the outer crust or cheese rind, and a look is taken to see if there is not too much if any cracking that has caused the air to get in the cheese, which will have given rise to blue mould creeping into the inside of the cheese.

Using either the edge of a thick piece of glass or a small piece of flat metal, the surface of the cheese is gradually cleaned off, and this is a fine balance, as not to go to deep in scraping away the cheese rind, or this can also cause cracks in the cheese as well.

Once the surface is finally cleaned or scraped off, a clear edible coating is then painted all over the cheese to give the cheese its show protection and presentation.

After this, the next critical stage is applying a white cloth to go all around the cheese, which must be as even as is possible, for this helps with presentation points in judging.

To do this for the cylindrical cheese makers, was although hard work with the other age classes taking anything up to one hour per cheese to prepare, and in those days of the late 1980's of Crump Way at Wells, and giving the then show rulings, there were then two whole matching cheeses per class, which made the task even more arduous.

Then of course there were copious inspections when the farmers and cheese makers were on site at Crump Way, and not to mention from time to time, the steely eye of Miss K.D.Maddever; pressure what pressure?

This way of procedures I undertook for several years, and was done over a week before the actual show, while for the new era of block shape cheddars, these were done at the actual farms of production, with each cheese being presented in a clear film wrap, and sealed evenly all over for its show presentation, with each to have clear sharp edges and corners.

My actual introduction to being on the showground of the Royal Bath and West was to be quite a baptism, in more ways than one, for at the time the cheese exhibits were housed in a wooden building close to where the Bee and Honey Section is today on the show field.

No sooner than I had arrived to do some stewarding, there was to be what we call today flash flooding, and such was the ferocity of the storm, the showground quickly turned into rivers down the sloping gradients of the site, and the cheese and dairy building was one of the victims of the day with torrents of water going right through the centre of the building.

A day never forgotten, more so when the car parks became oceans of mud; so in all quite a welcome to the outdoor pleasures of agriculture shows.

While outdoor events such as the counties agriculture shows are open to whatever the elements bring, the Dairy Produce Section of the Royal Bath and West Show has always been fortunate enough to be staged inside permanent buildings on site with the dairy products temperature controlled.

Like the four principal rules for cheese grading, the same goes for cheese judging being, flavour, body, colour and finish as the key criteria of each exhibit.

For the smaller cheese and dairy shows, it is usually one or two judges that are required, but with the likes of the Royal Bath and West and others of its size, the teams of experts can range from 10 to 40 people to assess the awarding of points.

While for many years the key types of cheese were Cheddar and the full range of territorials, as the 1990's went on the growing range of other buffalo, cows, ewes and goats milk cheeses necessitated experienced judges to assess this fast expanding range of products.

The majority of the judges come from backgrounds in the dairy industry, while others are from the supermarkets, often their buyers, along with a handful of genuine cheese connoisseurs, and occasionally some guest celebrities and notable chefs.

It was here at the Show, that I have met and worked alongside many notable and knowledgeable people within the trade, and after Miss

K.D.Maddever, there are Arthur Hamilton, Jimmy Wilson, Roy Swan and Marc Adams amongst others.

It was through Marc Adams overall, that I really got to know the finer points of grading and judging cheese, visiting many cheese making farms and also judging at some shows, along with Miss K.D.Maddever there must be something special about their Cornish ancestry!

For female judges, it has be Eurwen Richards, seeing her going head to head with Marc Adams is a real master class, while the dynamic duo of Val Bines and Chris Ashby are also a formidable force with their wealth of knowledge.

The latter two, I have helped as tutor on their Cheese grading and cheese making courses at Reaseheath College in Cheshire.

I was to be involved in one way or another for twenty years with the Dairy Section at the Royal Bath and West Show, right from the actual preparation to the final removal from the building.

To give the public and judges a change each year, myself and my team of fellow Crump Way workers, Bill Derrick and Ken Corp, we would always try and give a different lay out of the tables and cheese exhibits, culminating one year in an intricate pattern, that all walkways led to the centre of the room, such was the free rein we had.

One aside, I must mention very briefly, that one year after a pre-Show meeting, I sent Ken details of the forthcoming event on the Thursday in the post, while next day while starting a holiday, I was walking through the town centre of Falmouth in Cornwall, a hand tapped me on the shoulder, and if that was not a fright in itself, turning around to my larger surprise it was Ken! It's a small world as they say.

At the Royal Bath and West Show, education of farming and farm related issues have always been key to the fundamentals of the organisation, and the Dairy Produce Section has often brought forward many worthy projects, including that of the authors, 'Investment In Cheese Grading Skills' which we did in partnership with the Show Society and supermarket Waitrose, which we did over a two year period, visiting a whole range of cheese makers, cheese making colleges and even on the shop floor in Waitrose itself.

Sponsored by Nigel White's British Cheese Board, the Royal Bath and West Show also introduced the prestigious Cheese Industry Award, and for its first year of inception, this was to be awarded to Miss K.D.Maddever, a most appropriate and well deserved candidate.

At the first of what has been an annual event in the cheese trade, Amanda Streatfeild who was the then Chief Steward of the Show's Cheese Pavilion, was almost rendered speechless when one much respected lady gave another much esteemed lady, her faithful and trusty 'cheese iron', a moment of sheer emotion, earning a very long applause within the cheese building.

Having met Miss.K.D.Maddever many times over the years whether from her visits to the old Wells Crump Way site, or at the Royal Bath and West, it was a great privilege to work alongside this remarkable lady, and in 1998, I had the honour on two occasions to take her to "See her boys" as she fondly recalled, with trips to Cricket Malherbie and Denhay Farms, and to see her face light up in pleasure at all the major improvements that had been made to meet the ever increasing demands of the market place, is something I will not forget, yet alone, her sensory powers and observations were still second to none.

Miss K.D.Maddever meets the Duchess of Kent at the Royal Bath and West Show in 1992 with Chief Steward Amanda Streatfeild.

Grateful thanks to those days go to Graham Fry, then the Managing Director at Cricket Malherbie and the firms two long serving cheese making brothers of Anthony Villas and Richard Villas for a remarkable day, while the same in gratitude goes to then Chairman of West Country Farmhouse Cheese makers Philip Crawford and his wife, along with Amanda Streatfeild and George Streatfeild and their every faithful cheese maker William Parsons, for another remarkable day out.

Following on from the Royal Bath and West Show, it is on the last Wednesday in July, that Britain's largest cheese show is held, being the Nantwich and South Cheshire International Cheese Show, with its history dating back to 1897, and is the venue for over 2,000 dairy related exhibits, which in recent years have all been enclosed within a massive temperature controlled tent.

Like the Devon Show, Nantwich has excellent connections to road, rail and air, and equally water, with the colourful canal boats of the Shropshire Union Canal adding a unique backdrop to the fields of Dorfold Hall Park.

While there are numerous other cheese shows held throughout Britain, which the author has had the pleasure to judge at, such as the Cheshire County Show and the Royal Welsh Show amongst many others, we return to Somerset for the month of August and the staging of the Mid Somerset Show.

Situated near the town centre of Shepton Mallet, the show's history dates back to 1852, and has more than its share of ups and downs over the years, and it is another event I have been involved with for over 20 years or more, and with my late grandfather who was a keen gardener, entered the horticultural section for most of his life, with the family donating the Tom Green Memorial Cup, which is vied over each year for the best vegetable collection.

It was through the late Gordon Walker of Crump Way that got me involved in the cheese section of the show, which is a small family one day event when compared to the massive Royal Bath and West Show. The Mid Somerset Show is also known as the Shepton Show, and when I joined, it was going through a few years of decline, but in the late 1990's and early 2000's the show is in its ascendancy once more, helped in part by a free admission, generously supported by many local businesses.

Also in August, and over the border in Devon, is another two day event, being held on the Saturday and Sunday of the bank holiday weekend in the market town of Tavistock.

It is worthy of mention, because today's Real Cheese Fair which was born out of the Tavistock Food and Drink Festival, was one of the many boutique foodie events springing up all over Britain, such as at Ludlow in Herefordshire and Melton Mowbray in Leicestershire.

Tavistock's Real Cheese Fair, is the brainchild of Elise and Gary Jungheim, and for their suppliers of cheese and other related products that are given space inside the beautiful surroundings of the Town Hall, it is a rare opportunity to see some of the last of Somerset's cheese makers, all under one roof.

Unlike the regimented style of the other cheese shows, there is a great informal atmosphere to be had, and such is the spontaneity, even the author gets to be involved with cheese demonstrations and talks.

To conclude the annual show season, there are two more events, with the Frome Cheese Show, held to the east of Shepton Mallet in September, and while the former dates back to 1852, Frome was established in 1877, and for much of the time was held on the third Wednesday in the month, in accordance to the Royal Charter, with the Show Field at the top of the steep North Parade, while lower in the car park near the Market Place the Charter Fair is held as part of the Carnival week of events.

For the locals, 1998, many deemed the moving out of the town to a new show site at West Woodlands a mile or so away, would lose the intimacy of the often confined original showground.

I also had much to do with the Frome Cheese Show over the years, even going on to be Vice Chairman of the Cheese Committee, and for my lasting legacy in the cheese show arena, was with the support of the then Chairman, Geoff Barber, a former cheese maker himself, of Lovington Cheese makers, and Dr Glyn Stanley, a dairy technologist for the cheese starter company Group Rhone-Poulenc of France, as they were then called, gave backing along with cheese committees of Devon County, Royal Bath and West, Nantwich International, Mid Somerset and that of Frome to create the unique 'Grand Prix Award Challenge' being for best cheddar that gets the most points at all the shows given.

The award is still be given today, keenly fought over by all the cheddar makers big and small.

The last big cheese show of the year, is the annual British Cheese Awards, which, I already mentioned, I have been involved with since its origins in London, and in its early years was somewhat frown upon by the large factory creameries, but its new style of judging and entry styles were to become the vogue for many of the shows I have mentioned.

If Miss K.D.Maddever was a formidable force to deal with, then the same is to be said of Juliet Harbutt, who created the British Cheese Awards.

Unlike the static agriculture shows due to their permanent sites, the British Cheese Awards over their twenty years have moved around the country, being staged at many prestigious locations, though in recent years Juliets home village of Churchill lying between Chipping Norton and Stow-on-the-Wold, has been its base on the delightfully small village green in the beautiful Cotswold countryside.

The nearest the British Cheese Awards ever came to Somerset, was with an appearance at Bristol's Watershed complex in 1993, that is until 2014, when the Royal Bath and West Show's National Cheese Awards were to merge with the British Cheese Awards.

For the author, this was to be like a homecoming, having spent 20 years serving on the shows Dairy Produce Committee, and this return saw me judging, but more importantly all the commercialisation had been taken out, and replaced with just the original cheese exhibition, a point I'm sure the late Miss K.D.Maddever would have approved. All the retailers now had their own tented 'Cheese Village' just outside the building.

The whole ethos of the British Cheese Awards is different to the other Cheese Shows; yet over the years to come, many have changed to the style of the British Cheese Awards image.

While the judging is still done on a points system, and everyone assesses the cheeses in pairs, it is the cheese exhibits that instead of the once regimented lookalikes, which may be commendable in its own right, it is the actual cheese that counts and more so its flavour credentials and more importantly in our ever growing economical, times instead of whole cheeses if they weigh over 20 kilos, the exhibit can now be around 5kg and its given shape is not a priority.

Other positive aspects the British Cheese Awards have created, are various informal get-together's whether it is a Symposium for trade and cheese enthusiasts, or specialist cheese tastings, not to mention the Cheese Festival, a two day weekend event, which for many years has been held in the grounds of Cardiff Castle; while nationwide to get the positive message across to the public is the British Cheese Week.

One of the key organisations behind the origins of the British Cheese Awards is the Specialist Cheese makers Association, whose many members are very small when compared to the factory creameries of the multi- national companies, and have such over the years created their own Code of Best Practice, Self- Audit System, and more importantly SALSA (Safe and Local Supplier Approval), which is a stepping stone towards the more complex BRC (British Retail Consortium) audit.

While we mention such matters, it is reassuring for you the reader and the public at large, that all established cheese companies no matter what size, not only comply to auditing, but regularly undertake daily, weekly and monthly analytical testing, with visits from the E.H.O. (Environmental Health Officer), the Trading Standards and the supermarket technologists; all of whom visit announced and unannounced!

Distinguishable Guest LORD BATH at the Frome Cheese Show in 1999 with Peter Derbyshire on the left and the author on the right.

Looking back briefly to the first Specialist Cheese makers Cheese Festival, it was pleasing to say, that Somerset's Mary Holbrook, from Timsbury, near Bath, won with her 'Mendip' cheese, while over the years at the British Cheese Festival, both James Montgomery and George Keen were to win the coveted Best Cheddar awards putting the county on the map.

It also has to be said the Specialist Cheese makers Association patron in His Royal Highness Prince Charles has done much sterling work not only visiting members cheese making dairies and cheese colleges but has also attended the judging at the British Cheese Awards at Stow-on-the-Wold in Gloucestershire, while inviting back to his residence of Highgrove, members of the Association including that of the author.

Such has been the success of the British Cheese Awards, that other Cheese Shows were to become influenced by the style of judging and marketing, and it is Nigel Pooley from Wyke Farms, at Bruton who is to be credited in calling the cheese section of the Royal Bath and West Show, the National Cheese Awards, to compliment Nantwich and South Cheshire's International Cheese Awards, while for Shepton Mallet's Mid Somerset Show, theirs were to change to the South West Dairy Awards and for Frome's Cheese Show, were to be entitled the Global Cheese Awards.

Nigel from Wyke Farms, who have become the county's largest independent cheese maker, closely followed by nearby Barbers, have created some ingenious marketing campaigns over the years, including insuring Nigel's nose for a £1,000,000 ! (Mine must be priceless!)

The new style of judging has made all the Cheese Show's more open and competitive, for as I earlier gave the statistics of the Royal Bath and West being predominately farmhouse orientated and for Nantwich's International Cheese Show often going to factory creameries, there has now been a surge of diverse exhibits winning.

THE LAST CYLINDRICAL CHEESE MAKERS

To conclude this book on the cheese makers of Somerset, is what several critics and purists would say are indeed the very last of the county's true original and authentic cheese makers, creating the clothbound cylindrical cheddars as they have been made for several generations.

I have already discussed the Quicke family in Devon and the round cave aged cheeses of Ashley Chase in Dorset and given there are only five remaining as I write left in the county of Somerset, out of over a thousand such makers after the Second World War; it does make the future for the survival all the remarkable and worth fighting for. The latter aspect I can vouch for, while working for Greens of Glastonbury upholding many capacities in the small family business.

With the final closure of the Crump Way site in Wells, and the block farmhouse cheddar makers were able for a while to stand alone and compete with the factory creameries, the small traditional round cheddar makers, particularly the unpasteurised producers of the Keen and Montgomery families were almost discarded, had it not been for the intervention of Randolph Hodgson from Neals Yard Dairy in London and the advent of the Specialist Cheese makers Association and the birth of the British Cheese Awards and a small yet growing army of cheese and food lovers in the media.

Would anybody want to start in the industry in such times of change?, well yes there was, and in fact two new producers were to emerge with Times Past cheese dairy starting out at the village of Draycott, just to the east of Cheddar, being set up by Stephen and Janice Webber, who have been in farming for several generations, and over a period of time were to create a successful range of blended small cheeses, many of which were to go on sale in the tourist village of Cheddar.

Also in Cheddar itself, while there are seemingly endless shops selling various cheddars of all different sizes, only one establishment manufactures authentic cheddar cheese which visitors can view being made, and this is currently called the Original Cheese Company, and like Times Past have made a success with a range of blended cheeses, thanks largely in part to the skills of John Spencer who has revitalised the visitor attraction.

Of all these 'blended cheeses' the most successful for Somerset, was to be the creation of a' beer cheese' in Ilchester, to the south of the county, in 1962, created by local hotelier Ken Seaton and such was the popularity, other blended cheeses were created, and a small factory was sited, on the edge of the busy A303, and over the years such has been the growing demand the once behind the bar business is now part of the Norwegian company Tine BA, Norseland.

Blended cheeses come in a vast array of combinations of various cheeses and numerous ingredients, often to whatever is in vogue including the ambiguous yeast product; and of such these type of cheese you either like or deplore.

My opinion when assessing them, is to ensure you have the right balance of flavour of the actual cheese and counterbalanced by the same level in whatever the ingredient is; sadly for the lesser quality made exhibits I have tasted at cheese shows, the latter ingredient far too often masks the true identity of the product, more so when stronger flavours are added like chives, onions and garlic.

These credentials are the same for any smoked cheese with or without additives, and getting the right amount of balance levels of cheese and ingredients is paramount.

At the other end of the dual carriageway close to Ilminster, once the location for its Horlicks Farms and Dairies factory, lies the village of nearby Isle Brewers and the North Bradon Farm cheese dairy, which at one time was part of the Cricket Malherbie quartet of farm cheddar making premises, and today is the hard cheese production of Cornish Country Larder who themselves make a range of goat's milk cheeses.

So to return to the final five genuine round cheese makers, we will start with the Gould family of Batch Farm, who are based in the small hamlet of East Pennard.

Cheese making has been undertaken here for around fifty years, and as I write, the business is undertaken by Fred Gould and his sister Jean Turner, their father only recently passing away.

The thatched cottage of Batch Farm, is a typically idyllic postcard setting, far removed from the real stark world of today's environment in the cheese world and all the pressures it brings.

Such is the grandeur of the rural setting, with the nearby church recently restored, and the nearby manor house, and its white tepee's used for (a success in) wedding receptions, created by the cult success of the nearby Glastonbury Festival, gives the only inkling to the modern world.

The head cheese maker is Richard Honeybun, whom I have worked alongside for over 30 years at cheese gradings at the old Crump Way site in Wells and currently on the farm, as while as spells of making cheese here. Such has been the success of his consistent cheese making that between 1989 and 1999 Richard was to win nine tankards at the Royal Bath and West Show, surely an unprecedented achievement, while over the years the family have won many other cups and trophies at the country's various cheese and trade shows.

Women cheese makers are now such a rare occupation (to be had), largely due to the heavy work involved, and Jean Turner is to be commended for continuing this role.

Like Richard, I have known Jean for the same amount of time, and along with Fred, it is often refreshing to have a good chinwag about the state of the cheese industry; which for the remaining five traditional makers as soon as one obstacle is overcome, another seems to crop up, while the underlying factor is the financial returns they get endeavouring to try to make some form of profit.

It is not to say that the Gould family and the other traditional makers are removed from the modern world, for all are geared into the computerised world of technology, and they have all gone back to the fundamentals of marketing the cheese themselves not only to retailers and wholesalers but also to the growing rise of local farmers markets.

In fact it was at Bath in 1997, that the very first farmers market caught the image of the public's eye and the arrival on a former railway station platform was to start a major renaissance for a new style of food market which the Gould family and all the others quickly embraced.

While the county had many established Charter markets, over a period of time they also introduced Farmers Markets as part of the weekly open air events, thanks in part is due to Roger White and his Somerset Local Foods operation based in Glastonbury.

The Gould family and several others also began selling their cheeses at the more lucrative London markets, showing how diverse the business was becoming.

If the Gould family are one of the few remaining traditionalists left, being aloft on Pennard Hill, the Green family at West Pennard have been in production much longer on the edge of the Somerset Moors with the ancient Glastonbury Tor just to the west and the site of the modern Glastonbury Festival just to the east.

I have been involved with the Green family in more ways than one, as you will soon discover, and while at first it was grading and assessing their cheese, it was the time, when under John Green, that the family firm made what was to be known as the 'Second Great Pennard Cheese' as part of 1989's 'British Food and Farming Year' with a major agriculture event being held in London's Hyde Park, where the mighty cheese was to make one of its major appearances as part of a tour of the country.

The equivalent of about 20 ordinary round cheddars were to make this new creation, which when completed its manufacture and maturation was to weigh in at about half a ton in weight, and about three feet across and nine feet around.

I certainly recall the Hyde Park event, being a scene reminiscent of the outdoor music events held in the vast open grasslands, with thousands upon thousands of visitors attending, and it was certainly a feeling of being packed like sardines watching the farmers recreating a cheese making exhibition in their tented marquee.

And while there was to be a second farming event the following year, due to the major success, the saddest memory, which is alas still true today, that so many inner city children do not know where milk comes from; with answers often as from a supermarket, out of the fridge or out of a bottle, and when you ask 'what about a cow?', the blank faces are a concern, for many do not know what a cow is or even what a cow looks like.

The mighty cheese even went on its travels for a special service in St. Pauls Cathedral! While back in the West Country we had the pleasure and hardy task of displaying the cheese in the dairy section of the Royal Bath and West Show.

Unlike the sad demise of the first 'Great Pennard Cheese', the new creation, despite all its travels and handling was to meet a more refined conclusion, with myself and a small team from Crump Way in Wells along with John Green and his team, we had the pleasure of cutting the huge cheese up, and even today I recall how close textured the cheese was and the evenness of flavour, with a longer than normal, cheese wire made to cut up the cheese into suitable sizes.

When my position as grader came to an end, firstly with the Milk Marketing Board and its successor Milk Marque, I was offered the opportunity to work with the Green family, thanks to John's son Lloyd Green. From there on in, I would cover most roles from administration to cheese making and eventually going full circle once more into cheese packing.

I would also share many ups and downs of the family business, which were and are still relevant to many small family cheese makers.

The organic side of the business was built up by Lloyd Green, and was a growing concern, until it was to be hit by the credit crunch and the start of the economic downturn, but with the family always forward planning, they were to make Double Gloucester and Goats cheese to a consistent success, though getting goats milk could prove challenging at times.

Cheese Masters with Tom Calver on the left with James Montgomery at the Tavistock Cheese Fair in Devon

Though Green's and the other traditional cheddar makers were fending for themselves, the constant poor financial returns along with the ever increasing costs of animal feeds and the cost of materials for cheese making and packaging were and are still dark clouds hanging over the family businesses.

Against such an ongoing background, and with the family even having a small packing unit, there were times when most of the Green dynasty could be found, with myself cutting endless thousands of cheese wedges, with John Green occasionally vacuum packing the wedges, while

Lloyd's sister Sarah and her daughters Felicity and Harriet would label and pack leaving Lloyd and his daughter Becky operating the office, while Lloyd's wife, Margaret would come around and keep us all on our toes. It was really a time of 'all hands to the pump!' A situation many a small company is aware of and has had to employ.

"How many more?" John would often ask, to which I replied, "Just keep going"; and while we went through just about every emotion possible, the sad fact remained, that the business had to adapt to survive, and slowly but surely the creation of the Glastonbury Dairy came into being, with the merger with Brew Valley Farms, a neighbouring farm, about a mile away, creating another story in itself.

As the saying goes, the last people remaining put the lights out, and I was to be with Lloyd, the last two people remaining during the changeover.

As we near the end of the countdown of the last remaining traditional cheddar cheese makers, we come to the only three unpasteurised milk cheese producers, with firstly that of Westcombe Dairy Company, which is situated in a hamlet close to the village of Evercreech.

The business has its roots going back over a hundred years, with the notable Cannon family which I have dealt with in the earlier chapters also residing in the village, and it was the Brickell family that were the ancestors of today's small business.

When Wilfred Clothier wed Phyllis Brickell, he soon began expanding the cheese concern, while in the 1960's Richard Calver joined the business which by the 1970's they were originally making pasteurised block shape cheddars.

By the 1980's Richard and fellow director Christine Gore, who is the granddaughter of the Brickells, began to reinvent the business into their traditional roots, and making a return to unpasteurised cloth bound cheddars in a new purpose built dairy, which was devised with much help from Martin Biggs; whom himself was a former factory creamery manager and also the head cheese maker at W.H.Longman.

Today, Its Richard's son Tom Calver, whose seemingly endless energy and enthusiasm drives the company along, and the improvements to the standards of the cheese has been much approved, which I can certainly vouch for.

Sweeping the board by winning all the silverware and trophies at the 2000 Mid Somerset Show, was to be their grand entrance to the wider cheese world, and Tom has now taken the awards to other heights other than just shows, and like the Keen and Montgomery family have also won plaudits from the media and celebrity chefs and food writers.

James Keen outside Moorhayes Farm, Wincanton, Somerset.

Equally important in getting the Westcombe name and that of the Keen's and Montgomery across to the more food conscious they formed a Slow Food 'Presidium',called Artisan Somerset Cheddar with the aim of educating consumers about their individualities. The three not only attending specialist events in this country such as part of Tavistock's Real Cheese Fair in Devon, but going overseas to events such as Italy's Cheese

Festival in Bra.

The Presidia project is coordinated by the Slow Food Foundation for Biodiversity, which aims to promote such cheese makers as the Westcombe's, Keen's and Montgomery to save them as part of our world's heritage of agricultural biodiversity and gastronomic traditions.

It is putting this book together in such turbulent times for our surviving cheddar cheese makers in the county, that it is all the more important we do all we can to save our living heritage, and I now come onto the last two real traditionalists of the cheese world.

It is close to the old trading routes between Exeter and London, what is now the bustling A303, and the South Somerset market town of Wincanton, on the edge of the panoramic Blackmore Vale, lies the farm of Moorhayes Farm, and the Tudor farmhouse of the Keen family.

During 1999, the family were to celebrate their centenary of traditional cloth bound cheese making, with Stephen and George Keen, being the fourth generation to be involved in the business.

Along with Stephen and Jenny, and George and Victoria Keen, the next generation of sons are upholding the family name with Nick who looks after the farming side, while James is following in his father's footsteps in making the cheese.

'Stonebrash and clays underlay the soils which grow the grass to feed the cows, to make the milk, to produce the cheese' is often used as part of the Keen's message in marketing their unpasteurised farmhouse cheddar cheese.

As said earlier in the book, it was a pleasure to see their former cheese maker Jack Parsons doing the 'Cannon' style of (pressing) or cheddaring the curds, and while the actual farmhouse is no longer used for the manufacture, the cheese production has only moved a few yards across the road into the dairy in the stone barn (another part of the farm.)

Like young Tom Calver at Westcombe, James Keen is also one of the next generation of cheese makers I have seen come into this way of business, and having seen their parents and their grandparents, as well as others in the small world of cheddar cheese making, it is also a pleasure to see these new young cheese makers are also starting off their families, and hopefully in the course of time their children will continue not only to fly the family name but also continue the art of cheddar cheese making.

While I was not judging at the 2013 Royal Bath and West Show, the Keen family asked me to put my comments on preparing show cheese and entering cheese shows as part of a blog on their website; which in turn is just one of the many new forms of communicating to potential customers, which the Keen family and others have adapted to.

It was while on one of my monthly visits to the farm, that I discussed about a book on the areas cheese makers, more so with four local cheese makers ceasing production for various reasons during 2012 and 2013, that George Keen was also of the same opinion that now was an idea time to reflect and equally look forward to the future.

So we finally come to the very last cheese maker to be given a profile, and for food gurus and the cult following they have, it is appropriate we end with looking at the Montgomery family.

How often it catches my eye that food writers like Tom Parker-Bowles, when it comes to discussing traditional farmhouse cheddar, it is Westcombe, Keen and Montgomery that continue to get the plaudits.

Just a few miles westerly down the A303, from the Keens at Wincanton lies the village of North Cadbury and the home of the Montgomery family, whom have been making unpasteurised cloth bound cheddars here since around 1911.

The village is a delight, much built in the local Ham Hill stone, still having a village pub and village stores with the family's North Cadbury Court close to the church on the road to the farm and cheese dairy.

While, today the farm is a mix of arable and dairy farming, and spread over 1,000 acres, it is the brothers of Archie and James Montgomery that continue the family name, with Archie more involved with the farming and James dealing with the cheese.

I always recall their visits to the old Crump Way cheese factors in Wells, in particular Elizabeth Montgomery, their mother; whom I called Mrs Montgomery out of respect; and being a typical entrepreneurial farmer she always arrived with sacks of potatoes to sell, and equally how strong she was lifting them about!

As said with all the changes at the time, the unpasteurised cheddar makers had to fend for themselves to survive the changes, and as I have said earlier it is with thanks to the likes of Randolph Hodgson, Juliet Harbutt and a growing wealth of appreciate food gourmets that the family has survived.

Sometimes even a bit of misfortune, has been quickly turned into positive use, when a week before the British Cheese Awards, the family business were to be victims of a burglary, with over six tonnes of cheese being stolen.

The news was quickly in all the local and national media headlines, and incredibly also in the press all over the world! James in a local press report recalls, "It proves there is good in every situation. Our cheese was praised as being some of the best in the world and the publicity we got from that was incredible. It cost us £35,000 of course, but in the long run it has been worth it! The irony is that the thieves could never even sell the cheese and in the end had to grate it right down so that people wouldn't recognise it was ours."

The family did however go on to win at the British Cheese Awards and have done so many times since.

Before their current cheese maker Stephen Bridges and his small team, the firm was noted for their former head cheese maker who was Harold Chase, whom I met many times, and again through the powers of the media, he was associated with the sounds of classical music filling the dairy!

If the likes of food and drink connoisseurs like Oz Clarke and Jilly Goolden were to be around at our cheese gradings, and even the venerable Juliet Harbutt, we think they would be proud of our descriptions of the individual cheeses, and that is what makes the unpasteurised cheese makers different from the pasteurised cheddars; for often as not each vat of cheese has different characteristics.

On a visit to Montgomery's in 2013, James, Stephen and myself were to be filmed as part of the *Hairy Bikers* (Dave Myers and Simon King) 'Best of British' television series, with the programme dealing with the topic 'Dairy'.

As I near the end of this book on the highs and lows of the current cheddar cheese makers of the county, and given that I have endeavoured to keep purely to facts and only highlighted the occasional myths surrounding cheddar cheese, and as I said earlier I had proposed to get this into print for the new millennium, particularly with the ending of the Milk Marketing Board and its successor Milk Marque, we all knew at the time the bubble would burst with the start of the credit crunch.

With this in mind and the predictions of the likes of the New Economics Foundations and others on the way we shop and the effects on our streets, this was also to have an impact on cheese making and marketing the product, for during a recent talk entitled 'Creative High Street' the national retail trade turnover is £303billion per week, with 58%

of the national spend in supermarkets, while Somerset has seen a drop of 7,000 shops in the area since 2002.

Whether anything constructive other than cosmetics will come out of the celebrity-led Mary Portas (Queen of the Shops) Town Projects we will have to wait and see, more so with on-line shopping of the computer age growing all the time.

Among the many shops lost are small family-run grocers, specialist cheese shops and delicatessens, and if we use Wells once more, as a central point, as I write, the number of new supermarkets in England's smallest city, equates as the local paper 'The Wells Journal' rightly stated, 2,000 customers per store.

We have lost all the old fashioned grocers over the years, and the central Cheese Shop in the Market Place, once owned by Marion Shaw, whom I have known for many years, was herself the Manager at Viscount Chewton's cheese dairy which also went into the pages of our history books.

Marion and myself, were for many years, stewards at the Royal Bath and West Show, and we both shared a delightful evening as part of the Specialist Cheese makers Association as guests of Prince Charles at Highgrove.

I certainly hope our last delicatessen in Queen Street under Dan Holland will survive the current climate of change, and with Wells finally having its own Food Festival there are still glimmers of hope for the future.

So it is just more than super marketing pricing, animal and material costs and so on, that have to be considered, in trying to make a living out of cheese making, more so with free market conditions opening up with the ending of EU quota restrictions, meaning in very simple terms Britain will be deluged with cheap imported mass produced cheddar, which our factory creameries will have to compete against, making it even harder for the remaining farmhouse cheddar producers to market their premium handmade cheese.

I recall my last days with Lloyd Green, when we went along the route of the old Somerset and Dorset branch line, and given all emotional turmoil in the farmhouse cheddar cheese making world, seeing the wildlife in the countryside, that this route still goes through the heart of two of the county's largest producers of cheddar, namely Barbers at Ditcheat and nearby Wyke Farms at Bruton and over in the east of the county right through Moorhayes Farm, the location of the Keen family.

It is from small moments like this it all comes into perspective, and while this book never had a defined beginning it also does not have an ending, for it is ever ongoing, and hopefully the tradition of farmhouse cheddar cheese will continue on in one form or another. For myself I have been a part of the journey in more ways than one.

ACKNOWLEDGEMENTS

There are so many people and organisations to be indebted to, in the preparation of this book, and it is here I would like to thank the following who have helped in one way or another (sadly some have passed away to that cheese world in the sky) namely:-

Marc Adams, ,Alvis Bros, Maureen Andrews, Chris Ashby, Sheila Ashford, Ashley Chase in particular Mike Pullin, the Baker family, the Barber family, Sarah Berry, Martin Biggs, Val Bines, Stephen Bridges, British Cheese Board in particular Nigel White, Michael Chamberlain, Cheddar Parish Records, the Clapp family in particular Louise Clapp, Philip Cook, Ken Corp, Philip Crawford, Cricket Malherbie Farms, Denhay Farms, Bill Derrick, Devon County Agricultural Association, Stuart Dowle, Geoff Dyke, Robert Earnshaw, Frome and District Agricultural Society, Graham Fry, David Gillard, Martyn Gosney, the Gould family, the Green family in particular John Green and Lloyd Green, Arthur Hamilton, Juliet Harbutt, Randolph Hodgson, Dan Holland, Richard Honeybun, William Howe, Richard Jeanes, Elise and Gary Jungheim, the Keen family in particular George Keen, the Longman family in particular Richard Longman, Miss K.D.Maddever, Jane Maskew, Mid Somerset Agricultural Society, the Montgomery family in particular James Montgomery, Nantwich and South Cheshire Agricultural Society, North Somerset Agricultural Society, Simon Oliver, William Parsons, Dennis Patterson, John Plenty, Keith Plowman, the Quicke family in particular Mary Quicke, Miss Nancy Ralphs, Eurwen Richards, Judy Ridgway, Royal Bath and West of England Society, the Saunders family, Marion Shaw, Somerset Local Foods in particular Roger White, Somerset Rural Life Museum in particular Louise Clapp and David Walker, Somerset Year Book, Dr Glyn Stanley, Christopher Stilton, Amanda and George Streatfeild, Roy Swan, Philip Thorp, Stan Thorp, Jean Turner, Anthony Villas, Richard Villas, Gordon Walker, A.H.Warren Trust Limited, Malcolm Webster, Philip Welch, Wells Chamber of Commerce, Wells City Council, Wells Journal, Wells and Mendip Museum, Westcombe Dairy in particular Tom and Richard Calver, Western Daily Press, West Country Farmhouse Cheese makers, the Willis family, Jimmy Wilson and Wyke Farms.

BIBLIOGRAPHY

BRITISH COUNTRY CHEESES *by Pamela Westland* Ward Lock 1988

BUTTER AND CHEESEMAKING *by V.Cheke and A.Sheppard* Alpha / Granada 1980

CATALOGUE OF THE LIBRARY AND ARCHIVES Bath and West Show Society 1990

CHEESE AND CHEESEMAKING *by Glynn Christian* MacDonald 1977

CHEESE HANDBOOK *by T.A.Layton* Dover Publications 1973

CONNOISSEURS CHEESE GUIDE *by Judy Ridway* Martin Books / Simon and Schuster 1989

DAIRY STATISTICS POCKET HANDBOOK *By Dairy Co* Dairy Co 2009

FARMHOUSE CHEDDARMAKERS MANUAL *by Miss K.D.Maddever* Milk Marketing Board 1988

FARMHOUSE ENGLISH CHEESE *by Brenda Ralph Lewis* EP Publishing 1978

FORGOTTEN HARVEST *by Avice R.Wilson* Avice R.Wilson 1995

HISTORY OF STILTON *by Trevor Hickman* Alan Sutton 1995

HOOKED ON CHEESE *by F.W.Foukes* Shropshire Libraries and Cheshire Library Service 1985

ON FARM CHEESEMAKERS OF ENGLAND AND WALES Milk Marketing Board 1988

PRACTICAL CHEESEMAKING *by Kathy Biss* Crowood Press 1988

SHEPTON SHOW 150 YEARS *by Alan Stone* Creeds the Printers 2002

TASTE OF SOMERSET *edited by Janet Laurence* Good Books 1989

WORLD ENCYCLOPEDIA OF CHEESE *by Juliet Harbutt* Lorenz Books 1998

PICTURE CREDITS

p15 Steve Roberts for Western Daily Press

p19 Chris Ashby

p23 Keith Plowman

p27 and p57 Richard Green

p33 and p75 John Green

p37 West Country Farmhouse Cheesemakers

p47 Dan McCade Media

p53 Maureen Andrews

p65 Royal Bath and West Show Society

p69 Frome Cheese Show

p77 The Keen family

24 Forest Houses
Halwill
Beaworthy
Devon
EX21 5UU